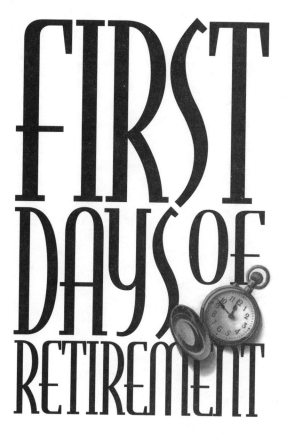

FIRST DAYS OF RETIREMENT

FIRST DAYS OF RETIREMENT

DEVOTIONS TO SET A NEW PACE

MARY HARWELL SAYLER

BROADMAN
&HOLMAN
PUBLISHERS

Nashville, Tennessee

4253-90
0-8054-5390-3

Dewey Decimal Classification: 242.65
Subject Heading: Devotional Literature \ Retirement
Library of Congress Card Catalog Number: 95-12241

Scripture quotations are from the AMP, The Amplified Bible, Old Testament © 1965, 1987, by The Zondervan Corporation and the New Testament © The Lockman Foundation 1958, 1987, used by permission; NIV, the Holy Bible, New International Version, © 1973, 1978, 1984, by International Bible Society; NKJV, New King James Version, © 1982, Thomas Nelson, Inc., Publishers; NRSV, New Revised Standard Version of the Bible, © 1989, by the Division of Christian Education of the National Council of the Churches of Christ in the United States of America, used by permission, all rights reserved; REB, The Revised English Bible, © Oxford University Press and Cambridge University Press, 1989, reprinted by permission (this is a revision of the New English Bible; the New Testament was first published by the Oxford and Cambridge University Presses in 1961, and the complete Bible in 1970).

Library of Congress Cataloging-in-Publication Data
Sayler, Mary Harwell.
    First days of retirement : devotions to set a new pace/ Mary Harwell Sayler
        p.   cm.
    ISBN 0-8054-5390-3 (pbk.)
    1. Retirees—Prayer-books and devotions—English. 2. Aged—Prayer-books and devotions—English. 3. Devotional calendars. 4. Spiritual life—Christianity.
    I. Title.
    BV4596.R47S28   1995
    242'.65—dc20   95-12241
                                                          CIP

99 98 97 96 95 5 4 3 2 1

To you who have shown me
the many blessings and
creative possibilities of retirement
and ageless strengths
that do not decline,
I thank you—
and God.

I've been blessed by
the long, productive lives
of my father's mother,
Mary Palestine Fitzgerald Harwell,
and my mother's sister,
Lucile Angel Henegar:
two strong women who loved
and welcomed me as a child
and as an adult too.

I'm also grateful for the strong faith,
spiritual depth, and insight
of my aunt, Evelyn Angel Miller;
for the strong character
and caring of my husband's aunt,
Evelyn Green Connell;
and for the strong family devotion
and remarkable resiliency
of my uncle and aunt,
John D. and Mary Anna Fitzgerald.

God bless
each of them
—and you—
as you begin your
first days of retirement.

Introduction

Congratulations! You've just become part of a select group who's unemployed on purpose! You probably won't need an alarm clock now to arrive at work on time. To get up and going, however, quickly establish a new routine. From your very first days of retirement, begin each day with God. Seek His presence and power in regular times of prayer, Bible study, and daily devotion to His Word. Let Him speak with you in these first days of retirement and all the years to come.

As you begin this devotional journey, release your time, talents, relationships, and dreams into God's care. Give Him your thoughts and feelings too. Then you'll be able to hear and receive His personal word for you—an "inner knowing" or inspired thought, a word from the church, or circumstances that He's arranged to lead you. Each must rest comfortably in God's written Word, so get to know the Bible well by daily reading a translation you especially prefer.

You have many excellent choices; but in these pages you'll find Scripture from the Amplified Bible, the New International Version, the New King James Version, the New Revised Standard Version of the Bible, and the Revised English Bible.

As you begin these blessed years of your life, rejoice in the time to enjoy each day. Begin a new phase of growing in your relationships with others and especially in your relationship with God. Let these first ninety days start you on a fresh journey with Him.

Day 1

This is the day the LORD has made;
We will rejoice and be glad in it.

Psalm 118:24, NKJV

Something strange has happened. This morning you woke up realizing, *I don't have to go to work today. I don't have to go to work—ever!* How you feel about this depends on many things, such as the quality of work you left behind or the health, energy, and enthusiasm you bring to retirement.

If you loved your career, you'll need new challenges. However, if personal relationships, hopes, dreams, and self-esteem were often displaced by your former position, you can reposition yourself to enjoy them now. If your old job primarily provided disappointment, you can work through and retire those regrets as you pray and journal in these pages.

Although you've terminated your employment, you're not unemployed from life. Your former occupation no longer occupies you, but something else will. This "something else" might not generate income but out-go—outgoing use of the interests, energy, talents, and experiences God put to work in you and employs in you still.

As you reach retirement, welcome this opportunity to clean out your job files! Be glad to resolve what's past so you can go into your present daily task of seeking, finding, and following God. Job fears or failures needn't follow you. These, too, can be retired as you enjoy a restful time—a new beginning and permanent place of employment in God's kingdom. So rejoice! The Lord has made this day—your first day of retirement—to work for your good.

Prayer: Dear Heavenly Father, thank You for this day You've made—even though I have mixed feelings about it! Please help me to let go of every disappointment, fear, or failure about my work or myself, but help me also to relinquish each success to You. Sometimes I did well; sometimes I didn't. Now I need You to help me know that I am not the job I've left behind. I am not my own work. I'm Yours in Jesus' name.

Journey with God: Rejoice in this blessed rest from labor by putting to rest any unresolved issues at work in you. Ask God to come into hurtful memories, disappointments, or failed goals that hinder you from relaxing and being at peace. Thank Him for continuing to quiet, heal, strengthen, and forgive you. Ask how He'd like for you to rejoice in His ceaseless but untiring work. Then listen to the thoughts, feelings, and Scripture He brings to your mind, taking note of them in the space provided each day for your journaling.

_____

_____

_____

_____

_____

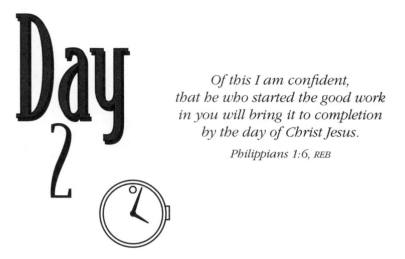

Day 2

*Of this I am confident,
that he who started the good work
in you will bring it to completion
by the day of Christ Jesus.*

Philippians 1:6, REB

Do you feel as though you've started the vacation of a lifetime? In some ways, you have. You've begun a time of rest from old responsibilities and duties. You've also begun a life of relaxation as you rest more and more fully in God's will. Don't think, though, that retirement brings a long time of do-nothingism or a ceaseless *vacation* from life!

A vacation is an outing in which you "get away from it all." If you vacate the premises—or at least the premise of work—maybe you will take that trip to Europe or the Holy Lands, but maybe not. Maybe you'll be eager to stay home and enjoy a renewed working place within yourself and God.

Years before you began your first job, your Heavenly Father started His good work in you. Although you've retired, He hasn't! He hasn't finished with you. He hasn't come again in person, nor have you taken permanent residence in heaven. But you belong to Him through Christ and will one day be whole and complete in His presence. Meanwhile, you can be confident that, at home or away, God will continue His work in you until you're fully and completely the person He created you to be.

If your former job was an extension of yourself, maybe you're wondering just who you are now. As a Christian, you're a unique extension of God's self. You're exactly who He wants and what He needs as He labors on your behalf, achieves His goals, supplies His Spirit, and blesses His work in and through you. So relax! Take it easy. Take a nap, but keep your eyes open! Retirement is no vacation! It's time to retire your work and rest fully in the Lord so He can get on with *His* good work—the eternal life of Christ in you.

Prayer: Dear God, I thought retirement meant a long vacation and no work! Now I see it's a time of renewal. Help me to rest in You and know without a doubt that Your holy work still works in me in Jesus' name.

Journey with God: Ask God to show you areas in which you have resisted His work in your life. Talk with Him about changes to make and directions to take toward His good work in you.

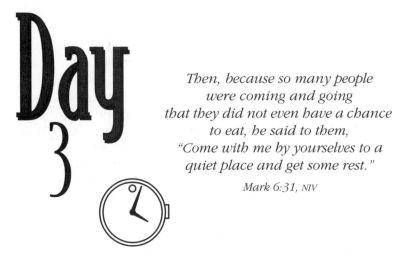

Then, because so many people
were coming and going
that they did not even have a chance
to eat, he said to them,
"Come with me by yourselves to a
quiet place and get some rest."

Mark 6:31, NIV

Did you have to train someone to do your job before you could retire? Perhaps you sold a business and had to help the new owners through the transition. Maybe you felt urged to write an instructional manual to tell your replacement about the details involved in your old job. You had to sort through a work area, file system, or tool box too. Maybe you showed your surprise at a retirement party held in your honor. For weeks, you've probably been a very, very busy person, but now what?

Now is the time to retire from busy-ness. Now is the time to be quiet and rest. Now is the time to take nourishment in the Lord as you hear His call, "Come with Me *by yourself.*" For such a personal meeting, you don't need a briefcase, portfolio, prospectus, or any other prop or tool—not necessarily even a Bible! It's just you and God getting together, quietly and restfully, away from the busy-ness of the business world.

The more you've had to do, the harder it may be for you to come empty-handed. If you're used to being the person in charge, you may have forgotten how to rest. Maybe you don't remember what a quiet place is, much less where to find one! If so, sit down. Get comfortable. Put up your feet and just be still. Don't do anything.

Don't even say anything, except perhaps, "Here I am, Lord. I've come to be with You."

Maybe you'll sit there all afternoon. Maybe you'll doze off. Maybe you'll be distracted by your own thoughts. Yet as you gradually come into the fullness of this quiet, you'll retire in the tireless, timeless strength of Psalm 46:10, "Be still, and know that I Am God" (NKJV).

Prayer: Dear Father, I'm so used to being busy and active, I've forgotten how to rest quietly in You. I need Your help, Lord. Show me how to just *be* in You in Jesus' name.

Journey with God: Talk with God about the distractions around you. Offer to Him in prayer each person, activity, thought, or emotion that comes to you during this quiet time.

Day 4

So they went away by themselves in a boat to a solitary place.

Mark 6:32, NIV

Hey, guess what? The Bible advocates taking a cruise! Perhaps it does—especially if that's what it takes to get you away from a car phone, fax machine, doorbell, or television set!

If you're blessed with a Christian spouse, the two of you might need to get away by yourselves for a while. This could return your romance to the high seas or renew your awareness of each other on a picnic aboard a pontoon boat. A ferry ride to the Statue of Liberty or a canoe trip on a slowly moving river can be a great way to rekindle an old flame or spark in a marriage. The purpose of this cruise isn't to bring your love life out of retirement, however! It's meant to retire your life's love into God, away from daily distractions.

Whether you're married, widowed, divorced, or single, begin your first days of retirement by discovering God's personal will for you. This differs for each individual, but any course charted by God ultimately leads to Him. As pursuit of God's will becomes your port of call, you'll venture into His presence. You'll "get away" to the restful, solitary place He prepared for you, long before your busy life began.

For such a profound journey, bring along every piece of luggage you've been lugging around so you can toss it overboard in prayer! Not only will you be free of excess baggage, you'll be able to catch God's lifeline of forgiveness. That might not make this the most pleasant cruise you will ever take or the least expensive! This cruise could cost you a bundle! It costs everything you've ever done, everything you've ever owned, and everything you've ever been. It takes you for all you're worth! Yet it exchanges your worth for the worthiness of Christ, paid in full by Him.

Prayer: Dear God, it's so hard to let go! Help me to release to You the burdens of the past. Help me to repay every wrong with Your forgiving love. Help me to be at peace with other people and myself, but especially with You in Jesus' name.

Journey with God: In this space, toss burdensome anxieties or resentments overboard in prayer. Keep current in forgiveness. Let God buoy your faith as He navigates you into deep, living waters that flow only from Him.

_____

_____

_____

_____

_____

_____

_____

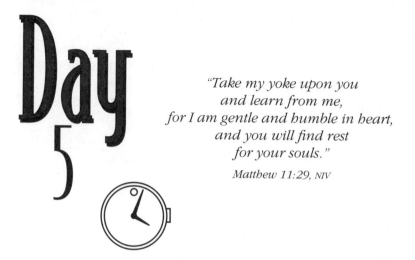

Day 5

*"Take my yoke upon you
and learn from me,
for I am gentle and humble in heart,
and you will find rest
for your souls."*

Matthew 11:29, NIV

Isn't it great? You no longer have to punch a time clock or go to a job you dislike. You no longer have to face heavy competition, career demands, or the expectations placed on you to provide a certain salary or perform a certain job. You don't have to worry about pleasing coworkers, employees, employers, clients, or irate customers. You don't have to meet a sales quota or a production level. Very possibly you don't have to do much of anything!

If you've spent years harnessed to a job, especially one you didn't like, you probably just want to enjoy your freedom now. You might feel hesitant to take on any new commitment for fear of being trapped again or badly yoked—and no wonder! However, you needn't fear the yoke of Christ. In these first freeing days of retirement, let Him lead you into a recollection of the person you may have forgotten even existed. Remember? Can you recall who you were as a child, youth, or young adult? Can you remember what you once expected to be or who you thought you were before *work, work, work* changed you into someone else? Can you recognize yourself? Maybe not! If it's been a while since you experienced fellowship with God, you may have become a stranger to yourself. Yet not to Him; God knows who you are. So trust His Holy Spirit to remind you. Trust yourself to His well-fitted, nonchafing yoke—His harness for your energy and talent—custom-made for you in the presence, power, and perfect fit of Jesus' gentle name.

Prayer: Dear Heavenly Father, thank You for never forgetting who I am in You. Help me, humbly and happily, to accept Your perfect will for me in Christ Jesus.

Journey with God: Who do you think you are? Would God agree? In Christ, how does He see you? Talk with Him about misshapen views you have of yourself or His love.

_____

_____

_____

_____

_____

_____

_____

_____

_____

_____

_____

Day 6

There remains, then, a Sabbath-rest for the people of God; for anyone who enters God's rest also rests from his own work, just as God did from his.

Hebrews 4:9–10, NIV

Have you let go of your job yet? The more you enjoyed your work—the more satisfied or gratified your career made you feel—the harder it may be to relinquish your position now. Maybe you feel angry about being pushed out the door too soon. Maybe you feel resentful toward those who took over your company or position. Maybe you wished you'd done more, earned more, or had more influence on the people around you. Whether filled with regret or relief, you probably feel somewhat grieved. A major portion of your life has ended with only a glimpse toward the new life you will soon experience. With the demise of your working life as you know it, you may feel as though a loved one has died. You may even need to have a good cry! You would if this grief were for someone you loved, and it is—yourself. You've suffered some measure of loss as you lay part of yourself aside, perhaps forever. So . . . cry, grieve, and acknowledge your feelings even if you're happy to be in a better resting place. As you release these sorrows about your former career, you'll be more apt to rest peacefully.

When God finished His creative work, He rested. He took a sabbatical or Sabbath-rest not because He was tired, but because He'd finished what He'd set out to do.

Too soon He grieved over sin that marred His creation. Yet for a little while, He could enjoy the good He'd accomplished—and so can you! Enjoy God's ongoing good. In this Sabbath-rest, listen to His voice saying, "Let it be," as He lays your old work to rest and calls forth His newly created life in you.

Prayer: Dear Creator God, I don't always hear You well. I don't always hear myself or my own feelings! Help me to let go of the grief and loss I'm experiencing. Help me to rest from my work in the peace and passion of Christ's name.

Journey with God: On this page, tell God how you feel. Rest your thoughts and emotions in Him.

Day 7

To everything there is a season,
A time for every purpose
under heaven.

Ecclesiastes 3:1, NKJV

In the beginning, God created time. Then He divided it. With day and night clocking in routinely, humankind saw the distinction between work and rest. People found themselves in a twenty-four-hour cycle where they could alternate between seeing clearly and clearly being in the dark!

In the beginning of your career, you created a time, place, and space for your work. You established priorities, separating the significant from the insignificant, the urgent from the not-so-urgent, the light from the load. Clearly you saw a division of work and the need to use that productive time well; when it was over, you retired.

So what use is time to you now? What good is it without something worthwhile to do? What divides one day from the next? And why does the night last so long?

With lights out, there's darkness—and that's good! It's a time to rest, reflect, and listen as the voice of God speaks to you in the quiet retirement of the night. For you, this silent night may not be a once-in-a-lifetime evening. In God's holiness, you may find an eve of recollection, renewal, relaxation, and repose. In God's blessing, darkness becomes a time of waiting—not passively, but reflectively as you devote yourself to meditating on His Word. In prayer and journaling you speak with God more clearly and, more clearly, you hear. You rest your worries, work, and concerns in Him as though they're void of any power but God's creative work: *to bring forth good.* As you spend time with Him in thanksgiving, devotion, prayer, and Bible reading, you actively wait for God to make known His purpose, His call, and His division of work in you. So get ready! Let this be *His time* of your life.

Prayer: Creative Lord, thank You for using darkness to bring forth more of Yourself in me in the light of Jesus' name.

Journey with God: As you retire for the evening, the morning, or the whole day, reflect on God's light. Thank Him for dark times when He's clearly made Himself known to you through His Son, His Word, and His Holy Spirit.

_____

_____

_____

_____

_____

_____

_____

_____

A time to be born,
And a time to die.

Ecclesiastes 3:2a, NKJV

"Have you been born again?" Christians often ask that rather personal spiritual question, while people who believe in reincarnation want to know how many times you've died!

In these first days of retirement, you might feel that you're closer to death than birth. Maybe you wonder if life is worth living, or, worse, maybe you're afraid you won't get a chance to find out. No one but God truly knows what your future will bring. However, His Word promises you a spiritual birth in Christ—a life that never dies.

Here's the way God's plan works: Before you were even born, you were dead! Spiritually, mankind had already died before the first baby ever arrived. So the only chance you have for spiritual survival is that God sent His sinless Son to die for you. Jesus Christ overcame death perfectly, once and for all. He arose from His death and from yours—not again and again, but simply forever. In this whole and perfect love, God exchanged His life for yours. He gave you His holiness and spiritual life in return for your sin and death.

Have you done that? Have you given Him everything that kills you? Have you handed over every single sin, flaw, mistake, mishap, misdeed, misunderstanding, trespass, crime, error, fault, botch, blunder, or false judgment? Have you exchanged your (or anyone else's) misconceptions about you for God's conception of who and what you are in Him?

If you haven't already done so, put your spiritual death to death forever by accepting Jesus Christ as Savior. Be born of the Holy Spirit by your faith in Christ. Then you have nothing to fear—not life nor death nor fear itself! Now and throughout all eternity, you are alive in Christ Jesus.

Prayer: Dear Lord, I believe You are who You say You are. Help me to believe and be who You say I am in Jesus' name.

Journey with God: Talk with God about your fears concerning your life or death. Listen to His comforting, life-giving word to you. Write down what you hear.

_____

_____

_____

_____

_____

_____

_____

_____

Day 9

*A time to plant
and a time to uproot.*

Ecclesiastes 3:2b, REB

"Hey, Mom! Dad! Now that you're retired why don't you come live near us?" Before you even have time to receive your first pension check, someone might want you to spend it on a move! Old friends or family members will at least want you to come for a visit. So . . . ? Will you?

The more of yourself you've sown into your career, the more you may need to pull up now! You might find yourself weeding or reseeding personal relationships as you determine which ones need to go or grow. For example, you'll decide whether or not to keep in touch with people from work—assuming, of course, that you've already sent thank-you notes for those nice retirement gifts!

Most likely, you'll want to nurture family relationships—if not blood kin, then those in your church family or among Christian friends. You do have those, don't you? If not, it's time to sow! Just plant yourself in any church row in which you can align with the theology and bask in plenty of Son light. If that place happens to be different than where you grew up, so be it. Your denominational background isn't part of your DNA or genetic code! You're free to pick up or put down spiritual roots as God directs. If physical and financial health allow, you're also free to move across town or country. You're free to travel or stay put. You're free to be uprooted by God and planted on firm spiritual ground that's ripe for you!

Prayer: Dear God, I'm not sure I want to uproot anything or have any more changes now. Part of me wants to keep things the same, but another part wants something new to experience. Help me to reestablish contact with my family and friends yet not be transplanted just because they say "sow!" Help me to know exactly where You want me and with whom in Jesus' name.

Journey with God: As you talk with God, ask Him to quiet your thoughts and other people's opinions so you can hear His plans for you. Note each thought He plants in your mind.

_____

_____

_____

_____

_____

_____

_____

_____

_____

Day 10

A time to kill,
And a time to heal.

Ecclesiastes 3:3a, NKJV

Have you ever been accused of murder? Most people have! For instance, someone may have told you, "It just *kills* me when you do that!" or, "You're *killing* yourself with work," or, really deadly, "You're such a *killjoy!*"

Now that you're retired, you may be telling yourself, *I'm just killing time.* If you're resting or recuperating from years of work, that's not foul play! That's using time wisely to heal and mend. If you've been staying busy quilting toilet paper, however, you just might be killing time!

According to God's Word, you'll find timely moments for healing and for killing too. To discern the difference, think about this: What truly needs to be halted or destroyed? Take time again and ask yourself if you really want to put a stop to it or if you'd rather attend to moments that need fixing?

As you take an interval for healing, you help to restore your past, present, and future to the God-given time that is intended for you to work, rest, worship God, and enjoy His creation.

Healing times also help you to reflect on circumstances, emotions, weaknesses, and even the people you sometimes feel like murdering! These provide opportunity to rest your case in God and hear His side of the story.

Perhaps you'll recall an emotion or weakness you thought you'd killed but only buried. As you consider an appropriate time to heal or to hang it all, you'll see that only God can do either. Only He can make things right as He either halts evil or restores ill minds, souls, bodies, and situations. Only He has power to destroy or redeem. Only God knows the perfect, blessed, and holy time to kill or to heal.

Prayer: Heavenly Father, forgive me for trying to kill myself or others with unkindness, harsh judgments, and poorly timed words or actions. Forgive me for not coming to You in prayer. Thank You for redeeming me and my time as I retire each life-and-death decision into Your care. Show me what You'd have me do and how You'd have me pray in Jesus' holy name.

Journey with God: List *anything* you want to kill or heal. For each, write down the prayer that God brings to your mind to pray.

_____

_____

_____

_____

_____

_____

_____

Day 11

*A time to break down,
and a time to build up.*

Ecclesiastes 3:3b, NRSV

Retirement provides the time for you to have a break—not a breakdown! If you've been a nervous wreck trying to figure out what you'll do now, it's time to stop building a case against yourself and start breaking down each situation to a manageable size. So what's the big problem?

Maybe your apprehension or anxieties about retirement have been slowly building. If so, don't uphold those fears! Break them down by asking, "What am I *really* afraid of?" Then listen. Perhaps you're scared your retirement benefits won't benefit you very much. Maybe you're afraid you'll no longer be wanted or needed. Maybe you're frightened of being alone and ill or terrified of losing a spouse or loved one.

As you break down dread and worry, you have a decision to make. You can choose to build anxieties over and over again by telling yourself what's wrong. Or you can let each fear work toward building your faith in God as you discover what He has to say that's right.

To break down your fears and build your faith requires constructive communication between yourself and God. As you pray, you might write down your requests and petitions in a journal, dating each and noting God's response. As you read the Bible, you can look for

God's communication to you in His Word, which declares who He is and what He says. As you discover His promises, you can claim them on behalf of yourself, your loved ones, or other people God brings to your mind. Let His truths demolish harmful thoughts and build sound ones. Let His Word design the words you speak to yourself and others. Let God break down your fears and raise up your faith as you receive His communication of love to you.

Prayer: Dear God, help me to hear, think, and speak Your timely Word and thoughts in Jesus' name.

Journey with God: Do you ever tear down yourself or others? Does anyone tear you down? Ask God to help you give yourself a break! Ask for His thoughts on strengthening your faith and building strong communication skills.

_____

_____

_____

_____

_____

_____

_____

_____

_____

Day 12

A time to weep,
And a time to laugh.

Ecclesiastes 3:4a, NKJV

At the beginning of grief comes a distinctive time of mourning. If you left your work or coworkers reluctantly, someone probably shed tears as you said a final farewell. You at least *felt* like crying, but how do you feel now? Are you starting to get impatient with yourself for still sighing or being sad? Perhaps you or someone else has already said, "Get over it! Get on with your life!"

Unfortunately, during a time of adjustment, people often treat themselves or others with impatience. This comes as the mind thinks one thing while feelings feel another! Most people (including yourself) mean no harm. They want you always to be happy, but that isn't realistic for every one of the 8,760 hours in a year!

Without watching a clock or calendar, genuine love waits patiently, and genuine feelings feel. If you're sad, you're sad. If you're not, you're not. So don't lie! *Allow.* Allow yourself time to grieve, to weep, to sigh. Let this period of adjustment be in your time, not anyone else's. If that makes your family or close friends feel too uncomfortable, just head for a private, cleansing sniffle in a shower stall!

Sadness needn't drip onto other people, nor does it have to withhold memorably amusing times. As you allow yourself to experience your own emotions, you let in moments of laughter too: "Oh, remember that hilarious time at work when we . . . ." Without *living* in the past, you can *visit* it and bring your emotions up to date. You can and will adjust to retirement! You will, in your own time, accept the *present* of tears and laughter too. You'll get on with life—God's life in you.

Prayer: Dear God, praise You for being who was, is, and will be forever. Thank You for remaining the same, even as my life changes. Help me to release my tears and laughter into the patient love of Jesus' name.

Journey with God: In what ways have you or others shown impatience with your feelings and emotions? Talk about this with God. Listen to His response.

Day 13

A time to mourn,
And a time to dance.

Ecclesiastes 3:4b, NKJV

If you spent most of your working life in mourning, you probably want to kick up your heels now! You might feel like jumping up and down ecstatically or dancing with joy before the Lord. It's also possible, however, that you've listened to a daily dirge for so long that you're stumbling over your own feet instead of waltzing into retirement!

Whether you mourned or rejoiced during most of your working life, it's time to change the tempo. If a wonderful, exhilarating job has now ended, slow down a while and mourn its loss. If laborious labor has finally ceased, praise God and jump for joy! Leap out of bed, glad to be free. Enjoy the new beat—a lighthearted, light-footed rhythm in which you have been favored with a dance.

Like any old habit, the steps in a daily routine can be difficult to change. At first you might feel conspicuous or self-conscious about your footing. You might look too long at your toes or step on someone else's! That happens whether or not retirement is music to your ears. Yet eventually, it's up to you to select the tone to take and tune to sing. Step by step, you'll ultimately decide to spend your retirement in mourning or in dance.

The Bible says there's a time to mourn but also a time to have a ball! Either way, let God lead. Let Him get your first days of retirement off on the right foot, setting the pace and tempo that's right for you. Let His Word become your lyrics as you change tunes or tempo to keep in step with Him.

Prayer: Holy Father, help me to follow wherever You lead me in Jesus' name.

Journey with God: If you picked a song to describe your old job or work world, what would it be? Is that an appropriate choice now, or does God want you to change tunes? Ask Him to give you His theme song for these first days of retirement. What pace or rhythm has He set for you today?

_____

_____

_____

_____

_____

_____

_____

_____

_____

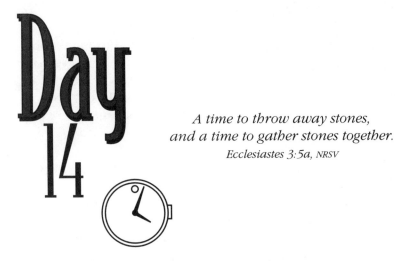

Day 14

A time to throw away stones,
and a time to gather stones together.
Ecclesiastes 3:5a, NRSV

The first time you receive a Social Security, pension, or retirement fund check, you might feel caught between rocky finances and a hard place! If so, you might be able to budge your budget by gathering resources and throwing away whatever weighs you down. For instance, you may be used to eating out but can no longer afford the cost. That doesn't mean, however, that you have to toss salad or fresh garden veggies from the menu!

As you consider your financial situation, think about what you can do yourself. For either necessity or enjoyment, you might find practicality and pleasure in growing your own vegetables. Depending on your available resources, this can be an elaborate set-up above ground in a sunny corner of your yard or one tomato plant in a patio container. Either way, plan the garden so you can easily reach plants—and weeds! If possible, gather food scraps, grass clipping, and leaves into a compost heap and let nature take its gardening course.

As you gather stones together for your retirement years, cast away those that have kept you walled off from nature. Rediscover the value of stones: stone-ground meal, stonewashed denim, stone walkways in the park, stone walls around a meadow. Skip a flat stone across a pond. Toss out the rocks from that new gardening plot. Even if you have only grown dandelions thus far, you're still capable of clearing new ground. (You kept a job long enough to retire, didn't you?) You're able to learn. (You're reading this, right?) So cast away rocky thoughts that say, "I can't!" Gather whatever resources you can from nature and look to God for every need you just naturally have.

Prayer: Dear God, help me to know what's needed and what's not in the nature of Jesus' name.

Journey with God: Are your finances rock-solid? Can you cast away debts or unnecessary items that weigh you down? Ask God to balance your budget; listen to the thoughts He brings. Ask Him to help you let Christ be the Cornerstone of all you build spiritually, physically, mentally, and financially for your retirement years.

_____

_____

_____

_____

_____

_____

_____

Day 15

*A time to embrace,
And a time to refrain
from embracing.*

Ecclesiastes 3:5b, NKJV

Have you been thinking about what you'll embrace and what you'll let go of financially? With or without changes, these decisions affect your ability to enjoy your retirement, depending on how well you're able to take care of your most basic needs, such as food, clothing, and shelter. When those vital necessities have been met, you then can concentrate on your less obvious but, nevertheless, very real needs, such as contact with other people.

Whether you're alone or not, whether you're sociable or solitary, you—like all other human beings—need to be touched, to be held, to be loved. From the moment of birth, everyone longs to be cradled and embraced. Sometimes that's appropriate, sometimes not, depending on the relationship or the persons involved. Some people also need more physical contact than others, but everyone needs an occasional hug.

Do you reach out and touch people with more than a phone or fax machine? Do you allow opportunities for closeness? Whom or what do you readily embrace? What memories, political opinions, personal views, or preferences do you especially hold dear? What spiritual beliefs do you hug against your mind or heart? What does it take to propel you into the arms of Christ?

As you come closer to God, you *refrain* from grasping old thoughts, old actions, old tasks, old relationships, old hurts, old feelings, and any old thing that brings you harm!

So first, let go. Then get a grip! Let God's Word, God's Spirit, and God's Son enfold you. Let yourself go—fully into His embrace.

Prayer: Heavenly Father, help me to refrain from anything displeasing to You. Help me to embrace Your Word and Spirit in Christ's name.

Journey with God: To what or to whom does God want you to be closer right now? Of what or of whom does He want you to let go, as you release that person or situation to Him in prayer?

_____

_____

_____

_____

_____

_____

_____

_____

_____

Day 16

*A time to seek,
and a time to lose.*

Ecclesiastes 3:6a, NRSV

Have you been thinking about looking for another job? Sooner or later, you might! Many people find that it's not easy to adjust to retirement, so they eventually reenter the job market. Maybe you will too. If that thought has already occurred to you, you might prayerfully consider placement through a temporary job service. Or let part-time employment or volunteer work help you bridge the gap between your longtime career and long-term retirement.

Whether or not you ever search for a job again, first look to see if *you* were misplaced in the one you had! Did you often "lose yourself in work"? Did you sometimes hide family problems, financial concerns, or even job dissatisfactions behind a guise of work? Did you lose a dream? Have you given yourself time to find what you've lost before seeking further employment of your time and energy? Have you looked hard to locate or rediscover what you enjoy most?

A blessed and timely retirement can help you restore what's been misplaced and also accept what's really been lost. For instance, every adult slowly loses his or her youth and physical endurance. Searching for vigor won't bring it back entirely, yet youthful attitudes can be found and wholly restored as you seek them in the age-less strength of God.

If you completely lost your financial "health" when you retired, you may need to seek an additional source of income now. If you've suffered a loss of mental health, confidence, or status, you might look for restoration or compensation in those areas. If you've lost physical strength, you might seek physical help. Whatever you've lost, seek God first. Find Him as the one true Source of all you ever need.

Prayer: Dear God, I don't like to lose anything! Help me to seek Your strength and find Your power in Christ's name.

Journey with God: Offer to God whatever makes you feel lost. Let Him find any parts of yourself that you've misplaced over the years. Write down what He sees and seeks in you.

_____

_____

_____

_____

_____

_____

_____

Day 17

*A time to keep
and a time to discard.*

Ecclesiastes 3:6b, REB

"Cleanup time!" If you and your spouse or a loved one planned your retirement together, one of you might be on a cleaning frenzy. Maybe you've already found your favorite cardigan or favored memorabilia in the trash!

"What? That old thing? Why, I didn't know it was so important to you, dear." That's the truth, and therein lies the problem! No one can know what's really important to someone else. Who knows what, when, why, or how much something is worth to you? Maybe you're not sure yourself! For example, do you know what that old resentment is worth now or what value you place on old anger you thought you'd discarded? Do you wonder where all those surprising feelings suddenly came from, or when that ancient wound will heal?

In these first days of retirement, declare a "cleanup" time in your life. No one but you can do it. No one but you can decide what genuinely needs to be kept and what finally needs to be discarded. No one but you can honestly say what's important to you at this very moment or to what degree.

As you free up closet space, you might run across old scrapbooks, mementos, and souvenirs, but you'll find good memories too. An object, garment, scent, or even an old LP of your favorite song may remind you of good people, good times, or good feelings about yourself. If so, keep it! Hang on to the joy—and maybe even that old cardigan! Just don't keep reminders of those old words that hurt or those old times that wounded. Dispose of them in prayer. Discard them into Christ's forgiving love.

Prayer: Father, it's hard to know what to hang on to and what to throw away. Help me to get rid of anything that keeps me from You in Jesus' name.

Journey with God: To let go of what needs discarding, ask God to come into each decision, feeling, or memory He brings to your mind. In the space below, take note of His power to resolve old issues and emotions.

_____

_____

_____

_____

_____

_____

_____

_____

_____

_____

Day 18

*A time to tear and
a time to mend.*

Ecclesiastes 3:7a, REB

Do you ever feel torn between what others want from you and what you want for yourself? If you spent most of your working life sewing up your own goals, plans, or business deals, it may be time to patch things up with your family. It may be time to make amends with old friends, neighbors, or members of your church. If you spent your job life working only to please others, however, it could be time to mend old dreams before they become completely unraveled.

In these first days of retirement, you've been tearing yourself away from your old job. You've been making needed alterations in your daily habits and use of time. Now, as you redress routines, you can allow enough fabric to include the people closest to you while adjusting the basic pattern of each day to fit you nicely too.

So how's your retirement shaping up? Did you shred all hope of employment before you were ready to rend yourself from the job world? Do you have bits of hope or scraps of dreams scattered around like squares for a quilt you haven't yet pieced together? Or have you allowed others to decide what you're to do and when, letting a pattern of people-pleasing emerge? If so, quick, tear yourself away!

Ask God to show you what pattern He has in mind for your retirement. Although this may mean pulling away from demands and expectations that have been placed upon you by other people or yourself, you'll sew up your ability to please God. You'll look to Him first to determine what you're to tear or mend. You'll soon see His unique, overall design that is perfectly suited for you.

Prayer: Dear God, I don't like alterations of my life! I'm sometimes torn between what I want and what others want of me. Help me to mend my relationships, but help me also to tear myself away from my own expectations and other people's manipulations of me to suit themselves. Show me how I'm to pattern my life in obedience to You in Christ's name.

Journey with God: Who has designs on you or your time? Talk about this with God.

Day 19

*A time to keep silence,
And a time to speak.*

Ecclesiastes 3:7b, NKJV

Mending relationships comes with practice of timely communication skills. Sometimes that means speaking loud and clear about what you honestly think or feel. Sometimes it means closing your mouth to keep from telling a lie!

Since God is truth, even those "little white lies" have no place in a close relationship with Him or anyone else! God is also love. Therefore, you can rely on Him to help you speak the truth in love. So what do you say? Is it time to speak of what you want or need? Is it time to tell someone how you truly feel? Or do you hesitate to speak at all, thinking that "a good Christian" would never say a single word?

Contrary to popular belief, Jesus did not spend His life "suffering in silence." As a person or occasion warranted, Jesus spoke, taught, clarified, and chastised. He upbraided the religious members of His family who couldn't seem to grasp anything He said or meant, and that, too, was appropriate. Yet Jesus also kept His lips sealed in a time of silence prior to His death. The people around Him only wanted to hear lies, so He kept the truth to Himself and carried it to the cross.

If you've been keeping the truth to yourself, you have, in effect, closed and sealed communication with someone. If you've often "let it all out," however, it may now be the time to retire old issues that others have tired of hearing about! Sometimes no one cares what you think, so there's no point in telling them. Perhaps you haven't known how to respond to something that has been said to you. That may be the time to be quiet and listen, but there's also a time for each person to speak and be heard. So give yourself and other people time to clarify thoughts and feelings. Especially, give God plenty of time to express Himself well in you!

Prayer: Heavenly Father, forgive me for speaking careless or poorly timed words. Help me to forgive people who have kept quiet when their words would have been helpful or those who spoke harmfully. Thank You for Your Word to me in Christ Jesus.

Journey with God: Ask God what He wants you to say and what He wants you to keep to yourself.

_____

_____

_____

_____

_____

_____

_____

Day 20

A time to love,
And a time to hate.

Ecclesiastes 3:8a, NKJV

How do you like retirement so far? Do you love it or hate it? If you feel a little of both, that's not unusual. In a love-hate relationship, people have trouble separating the two. For instance, if you hated your old job, you might have thought you hated working. If you loved your career, you might think you hate retirement now. Thoughts and feelings can get so jumbled nothing sounds too bad, and, yet, nothing sounds too good either!

To restore your passion for life, separate your thoughts and emotions. Be precise. Be clear. Be true. Ask yourself, *What do I really hate?* For instance, you probably hate violence, crime, unfairness, lies, bigotry, condemnation, and evils of every kind; but what do you *specifically* hate about retirement? If you're unsure, ask God to tell you. He will!

Maybe He'll remind you that you hate being told what to do, or you hate having no goals. As those issues become clear, you'll have a better idea of what you can do about them.

Similarly, God can help you to be more specific about what you love. For instance, He may help you to see that you love someone dearly even though you hate what that person says or does. He may help you to be more aware of what you love the most about Him—His unchanging truth, forgiveness, acceptance, mercy. He might even show you more about what you like to do and what you truly *love* about yourself.

Prayer: Dear Heavenly Father, help me to love all that You've called good. Forgive me for times of self-loathing and times of hating individuals instead of their choices, words, or deeds. Forgive me for failing to show my love to You, myself, or other people. Help me to separate likes from dislikes and discern an appropriate time to love or to hate. Thank You for loving me always in Jesus' name.

Journey with God: What do you hate about yourself or your retirement? What do you love? Ask God to show what you're to change and what you're to accept as a gift from Him.

_____

_____

_____

_____

_____

_____

_____

_____

Day 21

A time for war,
and a time for peace.
Ecclesiastes 3:8b, NRSV

"Wow, you're sure on a warpath!" Has anyone ever said that to you? Some things, such as truth, love, or justice, may be valuable enough to fight for. Others just aren't worth a war. Although most people will risk an occasional skirmish to get their own way, few will battle over a bias! Few are willing to die for personal preference or tradition. To go to war, you first need to know if it's worth the cost.

At the beginning of your retirement, you might actually need a good fight! You may need to combat depression, battle a weight problem, or attack a dilemma that's taken decades to arise. You may have to protect and defend financial resources or your level of energy. You might encounter assaults against your ego or your use of time. You might even find yourself in enemy territory as you confront issues that have caused family or church members to choose sides.

Hopefully, your retirement will bring a time of peace in which you can enjoy the company of family and the monetary rewards you've acquired from work. It's possible, though, that your induction into retirement will be about as pleasant as boot camp! For instance, you might have to boot a thirty-five-year-old child out of your house to encourage him or her to stand on adult feet.

Within your family unit, you may have to battle alcoholism, drugs, or sexual promiscuity. You may have to give up peace and quiet temporarily to wage war on unresolved issues and conflicts. Or you may need to declare a truce. Whatever you face, give up opposition to the command and leadership of Christ! Immediately surrender each person, problem, or personal right into His declaration of peace.

Prayer: Dear Father, I want Your perfect peace which passes all understanding. Help me to relinquish personal battles and territorial rights to You. Help me to accept Your terms for war or peace in Jesus' name.

Journey with God: As you consider waging war or peace, ask God what you're to leave within the domain of prayer. Ask what steps you're to take to stay in His close company within the boundaries He's set for you.

_____

_____

_____

_____

_____

_____

_____

_____

Day 22

*For there is no enduring
remembrance of the wise
or of fools,
seeing that in the days to come
all will have been long forgotten.*

Ecclesiastes 2:16, NRSV

Have you been back to visit your old office or place of work? Did everyone seem glad to see you? Did anyone seem a little uneasy having you around? Were you uncomfortable? Did you get the feeling that someone was wondering what you were doing there?

With salaried jobs still to do, some disgruntled workers might resent anyone who's retired. Others may envy you in a wistful way. Some might find your presence distracting, while others want to be sure no one hangs over a shoulder ready to criticize! Usually, most people just have business to attend to and don't have time to chat. So if you didn't receive the warm welcome you'd hoped for, don't take it personally! Do, however, take the hint: this is not your business now.

Sooner or later, most of your former coworkers will forget about you, but that doesn't mean no one cares! The people you felt close to will still be glad to hear from you—perhaps after hours or during a leisurely lunch. People who enjoyed your company might drop by now and then to see how you're doing, and newer employees might call to ask your advice. If you want to continue those relationships, it's up to you. However, you'll need mutual interests or activities to share with each person, preferably ones having little to do with work or retirement.

Realizing that your old position no longer exists may be a shock at first. Yet new faces and places will come as you make room for who and what you enjoy. Given enough time, most people at work will forget all about you! Given enough times of love and prayer, those you remember will remember you.

Prayer: Dear God, I didn't realize I was so dispensable! Help me to be winsome and welcomed everywhere You would have me go in Jesus' name.

Journey with God: Have you forgotten someone who needs to be remembered? Ask God to bring to mind anyone He'd have you visit, call, or write. Pray for those still in the workplace.

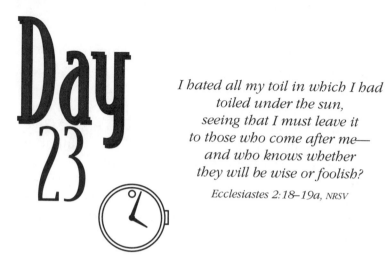

Day 23

*I hated all my toil in which I had
toiled under the sun,
seeing that I must leave it
to those who come after me—
and who knows whether
they will be wise or foolish?*

Ecclesiastes 2:18–19a, NRSV

*All those years I spent working so hard and for what—
so someone else could take over?* Most people feel upset
seeing other people in their old jobs, and maybe you
will too. If you're convinced that your replacement is an
absolute idiot, you might even be furious! No one wants
former success to fail. No one wants endeavors destroyed by foolish acts or decisions. No one wants life-
long work to become *invalid.*

If you once owned or managed a business, of course
you don't want to see it flop, but worse things can happen! Your former group or company could take a very
different direction from the one you worked so hard to
achieve. It could stop doing what you fervently believed
in, undo everything you tried to accomplish, and take a
course you don't appreciate or approve of, much less
like! What then? You accept it. You accept the sharp
ideas and dull wits at work, knowing it's someone else's
concern, not yours.

Accepting foolishness isn't easy, but neither is it easy
to accept wisdom apart from your own! A new owner,
manager, or worker just might come up with a workable
idea—one that benefits the whole company, and you
might wish you'd thought of it! You didn't, but that's OK.

You did what you did when it was your time to do it. Now it's time for others to try.

The past and the future come and go in your hands or someone else's. Yet only the present is at hand, so hand it over to God! Give Him your unsettling emotions. Retire the work you've done and the job others do now into His keeping. Ask Him to guide the foolish, the wise—and you.

Prayer: Heavenly Father, the dust from my old workplace has barely settled, and other people have already made changes! I don't like it, Lord! Help me to let go of not only the past but also the present and future, at work and in me in Jesus' name.

Journey with God: Thank God for continuing to bring good from all you've done. Ask Him to show you what you've done well and what you can do differently.

_____

_____

_____

_____

_____

_____

_____

_____

Day 24

For all their days are full of pain,
and their work is a vexation;
even at night their minds do not rest.
This also is vanity.

Ecclesiastes 2:23, NRSV

"Are you OK?"

"Of course! I'm fine, really. Why shouldn't I be?"

As you try to deal with troubling emotions about your retirement or former job, you may be tempted to pretend that everything's OK. Maybe it is, but if it's not, don't lie—not even to yourself! You probably just need to be quiet about how you're doing until you're sure what you feel. Meanwhile, the Bible speaks a timely word that clarifies inner conflicts rather loudly!

You may be amazed, for instance, to learn that vanity *awakens* insomnia! You might be dismayed to discover that remorse, depression, overactivity, and worry show futile thinking too. Maybe you'll even be annoyed to hear the Bible call painful thoughts or emotional pain vain! Yet honest thought and emotion recognize that each word of the Bible is true.

What's a person to do with such uncomfortable truth? Some lie. Some keep quiet. Some walk away. Some get outraged. Yet when the fury and upsets subside, God's people eventually see that He presents the truth for a very good reason: *So you will know what it is!* In comfort or in pain, your acceptance of His Word helps you acknowledge His truths about yourself.

God knows your anguish. He created you. He gave you the ability to think and to feel. He has the power you need to endure hurts or be healed. Yet, how would you even know you need healing if His Word did not make you aware of painful truths *beneath* the pain? How would you know you need God?

Prayer: Dear Lord, please help me to accept Your truth about what I feel. Frankly, I don't like being told I'm vain! I don't like to admit that my pride keeps me awake as I think about all the things I could have done or could change even now if I just put my mind to it! Forgive me, Lord. Help me to put whatever troubles me onto Your mind. Help me to let go of futile thoughts and accept Your work of rest in Jesus' name.

Journey with God: What troubling pain or emotion keeps you awake? Discuss it with God in this space. Ask Him to remind you to use painful, restless times as opportunities for prayer.

_____

_____

_____

_____

_____

_____

_____

_____

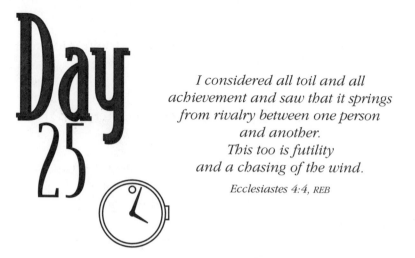

*I considered all toil and all
achievement and saw that it springs
from rivalry between one person
and another.
This too is futility
and a chasing of the wind.*

Ecclesiastes 4:4, REB

What a dynamo! Have you ever thought of yourself that way? Has someone else called you a powerhouse or a workaholic? If so, that may seem irrelevant now, but is it?

The more achievement-oriented you were in your old job the more difficult it may be for you to slow down. You're not alone, of course. Most people want to excel in their jobs, but this is more personal! If you have a son, daughter, or adult grandchild, one of them probably works superhard too! Most likely, someone in your family is also a go-getter. So here's the big question: What do you want to *go get?*

Although the answer differs from one person to the next, your answer might still affect you. Maybe you had a parent who often said, "You can do *anything* if you just set your mind to it." That sounds great, but it implies perfection! Only God can do all things wholly well, whereas humans must live with some degree of limitation. Or perhaps no one believed you had any ability! Maybe a teacher accused you of laziness. Maybe you wanted to prove yourself to a friend, sibling, spouse, or an entire community, so you told yourself, *I'll show them!*

For most people, rivalry begins at home. Everyone wants to be "the favorite" child. Some even carry this hope into adulthood as "good Christians" who try to earn points with God. Eventually, sin forfeits the competition, but Christ won on your behalf! So put rivalry to rest. You have nothing to prove to anyone—not even to yourself. God knows your mistakes and limitations, so He doesn't want futile denials! He wants your confession as you profess the victory of His Son.

Prayer: Forgive me, Lord, for futile ways. Help me to stop competing for attention or trying to prove myself. Thank You for not holding against me anything I place in Jesus' name.

Journey with God: Who or what is your biggest rival? Ask God for His insights. Ask Him to reveal what and how you're to pray about the competition.

Day 26

"For whom am I toiling,"
they ask, "and depriving myself
of pleasure?"
This also is vanity
and an unhappy business.

Ecclesiastes 4:8b, NRSV

If you were the primary breadwinner in your house, you probably worked overtime now and then. Those occasions might have conflicted with your family's plans, and so you may have said, "I'm doing this for you." That's partly true! Although you might have been coerced into working long hours anyway, your main goal was to provide for your family. That made your additional efforts worthwhile.

You might think all that's changed now, but it hasn't. As long as you have family members—child or adult—you care about, you'll still do what you can to help. The difference is that instead of working for a salary you'll use past and present income toward future dividends. For instance, you can talk with a reputable agent about the type of life and health insurance coverage you need. Also, ask your lawyer to help you set up a will and living trust if you haven't already. Even if you think you don't have many assets, you can protect what you do have from probate costs or other avoidable fees. If you own property or other valuables, talk with your financial adviser about estate planning. Ask for clarification of various investments and the potential risks involved in each type.

Although you've retired, your money hasn't! You can put it to work for you and use it to help others. Even if you have no descendants to whom you want to leave anything, you can still ask, *For whom am I toiling? To whom do I want to leave the pleasure of my labor?* Perhaps that will be your niece, brother, or some other relative. Happily you do have a say in what happens, so you just might want to say, "I'd like to leave a generous gift to my church."

Prayer: Heavenly Father, thank You for giving me productive years. Help me to labor, happily, for You in Jesus' name.

Journey with God: Is your will God's will? Is your living trust in Him? Ask Him about your insurance, investments, or other money matters, knowing that they also matter to Him. Ask Him to give you inner peace as He indicates what you're to do or whose counsel you're to seek.

Day 27

What reward does anyone have for all his labour, his planning, and his toil here under the sun?

Ecclesiastes 2:22, REB

Since the Bible asks what reward you've had for your work, surely you can ask the same of the Social Security office! If your former place of business helped to provide a pension or retirement fund, you might need to contact the manager of that program for more information. If you were self-employed, your accountant can discuss monies placed into an IRA or Keogh. Also you can talk with your financial planner about the payout possibilities from an annuity.

Retirement benefits vary for each person, but yours will depend, in part, on how much you planned for this occasion or were able to set aside. Your age and number of working years also affect monthly monies you receive and the health care or medical benefits you have. Your marital status and spouse's age determine your income too. For example, if you've both retired, you both should have some benefits from your working years. If the family breadwinner has died, you may be able to receive your spouse's Social Security benefits instead of your own, depending on which amount is greater.

To be sure your questions are thoroughly answered, list them before you inquire. The clearer you are about what you want to know, the more direct the answers will be. You may find exceptions, however, if someone just doesn't want to say! For instance, if your former company coerced you into an early retirement, they might not want to discuss lessened benefits. (Your lawyer will!) Hopefully, your years of planning and labor produced excellent dividends, so don't lose a single one. Ask direct questions. Get direct answers, and let God direct what's needed. Let Him give you the ongoing benefits of His labor: the everlasting reward that only He can afford to provide.

Prayer: Dear Heavenly Father, I praise You for Your perfect plan of eternal salvation in the name of Jesus.

Journey with God: What long-term benefits do you have as a child of God—in heaven and here, under the sun?

_____

_____

_____

_____

_____

_____

_____

_____

_____

_____

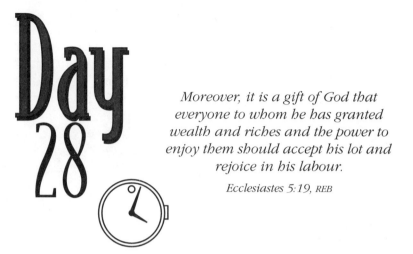

Moreover, it is a gift of God that everyone to whom he has granted wealth and riches and the power to enjoy them should accept his lot and rejoice in his labour.

Ecclesiastes 5:19, REB

Have you ever wished that you'd win the lottery? Have you thought about what you'd do with all that money? To whom would you express your thanks?

If you've been blessed with lots of property or lots of cash, you might have a parent, grandparent, or rich uncle to acknowledge. Maybe your spouse provided wonderfully well, or maybe you have yourself to thank! No matter by what means your financial gains came, you first should thank God. He placed possessions into your keeping and granted you some measure of wealth. So find some measure of enjoyment!

Rich or poor, welcome what you have received. If it does not seem like much, thank God anyway! The more you recognize, the more you realize what's yours. For instance, you must own at least one book or you wouldn't be reading this one! Otherwise, you have a library card or a friend who loans you books, so be glad for that. Don't wait for a winning lottery ticket to rejoice. Joy doesn't come from the cash anyway. It comes when the winners let themselves cash in on the en-*joy*-ment of all they have received.

Whether you've been given a little or a lottery, accept what you have as a gift from God. Accept your lot in life—and the cabin, condo, mansion, or museum on it—

as property granted from the King. With plenty of nothing or lots of everything, praise God! Acknowledge His gifts with thanks and, expressly, with your *enjoyment* of all He has given you.

Prayer: Father, forgive me for being dissatisfied with what I have. Help me to appreciate and enjoy Your wealth of gifts to me in Jesus' name.

Journey with God: Fill this space by thanking God properly for the property you own. If you don't appreciate it much, talk with Him about that too. Ask Him to give you His special gift of enjoyment.

_____

_____

_____

_____

_____

_____

_____

_____

_____

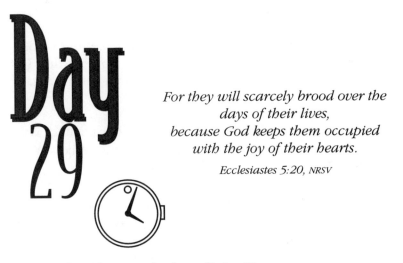

Day 29

*For they will scarcely brood over the
days of their lives,
because God keeps them occupied
with the joy of their hearts.*

Ecclesiastes 5:20, NRSV

"So what do you do for a living?"

"Oh, I watch soap operas. What do you do?"

Whatever *occupies* the majority of your time or attention becomes your *occupation*. If you watch television nonstop, that's what you do for a living! If you spend most of your energy thinking about what once was or what might have been, you may be employed in the full-time occupation of brooding!

Turning off your thoughts might not be quite as easy as switching off a TV, but it's as simple. Instead of using a remote control button, give close personal control of your thoughts to God. These Bible steps will show you how:

1. "Be anxious for nothing, but in everything by prayer and supplication, with thanksgiving, *let* your requests be made known to God; and the peace of God, which surpasses all understanding, will guard your hearts and minds through Christ Jesus" (Phil. 4:6–7, NKJV).

2. "*Let* the same mind be in you that was in Christ Jesus" (Phil. 2:5, NRSV).

3. "But you have been anointed by the Holy One" (1 John 2:20, NRSV). (Wow! Isn't that good to know?)

4. "Finally, beloved, whatever is true, whatever is honorable, whatever is just, whatever is pure, whatever is pleasing, whatever is commendable, if there is any excellence and if there is anything worthy of praise, *think* about these things" (Phil. 4:8, NRSV).

Because you believe in Christ, His Holy Spirit occupies you and can keep you well-occupied too! Your job is to *let* your thoughts be filled with His way of thinking. *Let* His mind remind you of the joy that awaits each day of your life.

Prayer: Heavenly Father, sometimes I don't know what I think! Sometimes I don't like my own thoughts. Help me to know Your mind and recognize the joy in Jesus' name.

Journey with God: What do you most enjoy? Ask God to help you recall the activities, relationships, or involvements that bring the most joy to you.

_____

_____

_____

_____

_____

_____

_____

_____

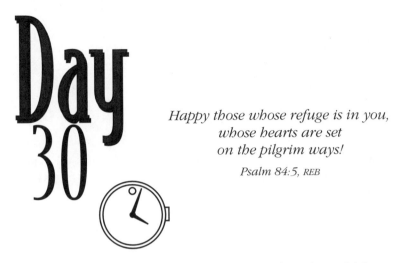

Day 30

Happy those whose refuge is in you,
whose hearts are set
on the pilgrim ways!

Psalm 84:5, REB

"You know what I've always wanted to do? I'd like to travel around the United States and see the whole country."

Why not? This can be a time for dreams to come true—especially if you're blessed with reasonably good health and low mileage! If you can afford to be away from home, why not plan an adventure while you can still budget the time into a new routine? Besides, getting away will often help you know what you want to do when you get back.

Even if the sky's the limit, you may not want to rocket. A motor home or camper will provide immediate accommodations in out-of-the-way places, and with an RV you can visit family and friends without inconveniencing them. If you prefer to "rough it," you might remove the rear seats in a van and replace them with a grill, cooler, and air mattress. Or "test-drive" a tent. If you're over fifty, you might enjoy taking a senior citizen's discount and whirlpool bath at a posh hotel.

Away or at home, you're on a new adventure in unchartered terrain. Unless you had a brief stopover retirement in the past, you've now spent your first month away from familiar job territory. If so, congratulations! You survived! Maybe you encountered some bad weather, rough roads, or close calls during these few weeks; but those needn't ruin the trip. As you continue your pilgrimage, you'll pass memorable landmarks of interest. You'll see fresh scenery and favorite places. Maybe you'll visit people you haven't been with for a while—old friends, family, or your innermost self. Close by or far away, just be sure to enjoy your adventure and leave your "driving transformation" up to God.

Prayer: Heavenly Father, I'm not completely sure what You've mapped out for my retirement, but I trust You to give me the signals I need in plenty of time to move it, park it, or take another turn! Praise You for ongoing blessings as I travel with You in Jesus' name.

Journey with God: Where do you want to go and with whom? Do you prefer for God to take the backseat or driver's position? Why? Have an honest discussion about this with Him.

_____

_____

_____

_____

_____

_____

_____

_____

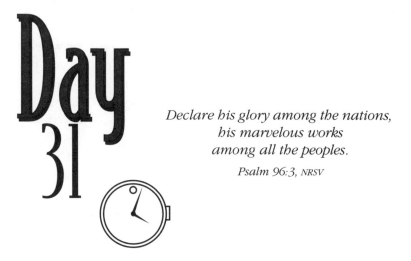

Day 31

Declare his glory among the nations,
his marvelous works
among all the peoples.

Psalm 96:3, NRSV

Do you feel persecuted? Don't you sometimes wish people would just go away and leave you alone? Maybe they're pretty obnoxious, but rarely do they persecute you for your beliefs! If you belong to a minority group, you might be discriminated against or harassed but probably not oppressed for your faith in God. If you're in an abusive relationship, you might be mistreated religiously but not tormented for the religion you believe.

In this country, people seldom experience persecution for their faith, but you might if you declare God's glory! It's a risk, but as you travel into other cities, states, or nations, tell of Christ's salvation to the people you meet. Speak of God's marvelous work in your life. Tell everyone everywhere about Him—especially friends and family—and see what happens!

As you venture into new areas of retirement, you'll meet people or situations that you previously haven't encountered. Some days you may not feel up to the challenge. When you do, however, you'll discover new friends, not just for yourself but for the Lord. Sometimes you'll meet people only for a moment, yet you'll find instant recognition of a soul. You'll feel as though you've known one another for years, and you'll glory in such friendship. You'll bring glory to God as you declare His loving work to *everyone* you encounter—even the ones who persecute you or those you wish would just go away and leave you alone.

Prayer: Dear God, I don't want to talk to people I dislike, so I sure don't want to risk persecution from them! Please help me to speak boldly of You in Jesus' name.

Journey with God: If you've ever been praised for something you did well, you understand about "getting the glory." Ask God to show you how that can be an opportunity to direct the glory to Him. Consider the marvelous works He's done for you personally. Whom does He want you to tell all about Him?

_____

_____

_____

_____

_____

_____

_____

_____

_____

_____

_____

Day 32

Oh, worship the LORD
in the beauty of holiness!
Psalm 96:9a, NKJV

"Hey, we're on vacation! I'm not going to church to-day; I'm going fishing. I'll commune with God on the lake."

If people really and truly followed that intention, they might catch more praise than trout! In the early morning sun, a mist drifts lazily across the water. A dragonfly darts about. A turtle glides down a bank. A fish leaps in a flash of silver and disappears in a splash. A pale shaft of sunlight glimmers through a stand of trees, awakening a choir of cardinals dressed in their best red robes. Slowly, the heavens increase their radiance, and, as light plays on the rippling water, the beauty of holiness streams by.

What church or cathedral could rival this exquisite design? What master planner could equal the skill, the diversity, the blessed sights, sounds, and smells of the great outdoors? Who but God could create such artistry to inspire the soul, the senses? No one! Yet, who but God would think of getting people together in church each week when they'd rather be doing something else?

Although the wonder and intricate balance of nature does indeed lift one's thoughts toward God, that's usually where the thoughts stop—within oneself. In a time of crisis or confusion, that may be what's needed to quiet yourself so you can hear God better. As you come together regularly with other Christians, you won't become a stagnant pool! Instead you'll pool insights, faith, and encouragement. You'll point to God as your Source of living water and together raise a waterfall of praise. You'll worship not nature, but the Creator and Lord of all. In His Body, His church, will you truly commune?

Prayer: Lord, thank You for creating my church for communion of Your plan and pleasure and my worship in Christ's name.

Journey with God: Did you hope to take a vacation from going to church? If you've been fishing around for excuses to skip a service, ask God to show what's needed for you to worship Him beautifully! Ask how you can freshen up the beauty of holiness as you plunge into pools of worship-filled times.

_____

_____

_____

_____

_____

_____

_____

_____

Day 33

O LORD of Hosts,
happy are they who trust in you!

Psalm 84:12, REB

Just because you're retired doesn't mean you're on the go. Maybe you don't like being away from home. Maybe you lack the transportation or energy to get to the grocery store and back. Maybe you're afraid to go anywhere by yourself. Maybe you worry about your car, money, spouse, health, safety, or all of the above! If so, be happy! You can't always trust yourself and the reliability of your car or credit, but you can rely on God anywhere, anytime.

That's what you want to do, of course, but some days you might be fearful instead of reliable about trusting God. You might wonder if He's really there or really cares about the little matters that matter to you. The more uncertain you are of His presence, power, or goodness, the less happy you'll be when those unexpected opportunities arise for you to practice trust. Yet unless you stretch your faith, you'll continuously stretch money, energy, and self until they are threadbare!

Something has to give! You can wear yourself out trying to take care of everything. You can fray your nerves and fret yourself to fragments. You can let relentless worries and faithless fears control your retirement like the employer who controlled your energy and time. Or you can just make up your mind to trust God.

By deciding to place your faith in God rather than in circumstances, you invite the Lord to be *your* Lord. You don't even mind your own fears or worries because you mind more what His Word says. You host the Lord of Hosts, happily, as you trust each occasion to mind your manner of faith in Him.

Prayer: Dear Heavenly Father, forgive my manner of showing displeasure in the hard circumstances You've allowed. Getting an allowance from You makes me feel vulnerable and no more in control of my life than when I was an adolescent! Help me to grow into being Your trusting child again. Help me to mind Your manner of gladness in the power of Jesus' name.

Journey with God: Are you happy? Ask God to show you what hinders you from enjoying His company and coming to Him as His child. Give Him each worry and fear in the space below.

_____

_____

_____

_____

_____

_____

_____

_____

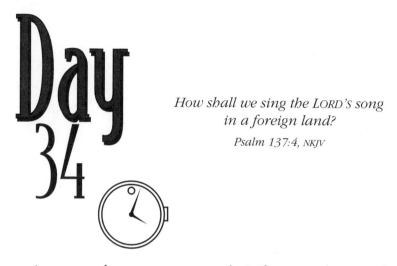

How shall we sing the LORD's song
in a foreign land?

Psalm 137:4, *NKJV*

Are you where you want to be? If you took an early retirement, you might be heading across the country, discovering places you love and others you'd rather not see again. If you didn't stop working until you entered a retirement home, you might be enjoying the new people and activities but without feeling either retired or at home. You may be wondering how to fit your possessions or yourself into such a tiny room.

As you adjust to the new situations that came with your personal retirement package, you'll feel strange at first. Each new circumstance will be foreign to your experience or routine. Some changes you'll like. Others you'll detest, but both bring a choice: to sing or to complain.

How can I sing in this strange place? How can I praise God in such a foreign land? The Hebrew people often asked that question, and perhaps you will too. Just be aware, though, that chronic murmuring got them nowhere! Instead of singing their way across a short, albeit inconvenient, distance, they wandered in a dry place for forty faithless years.

If your family used to sing on long trips, consider the advantages of doing that now. Rough times pass faster, making the trip seem like a lark. Attitudes brighten, hopes return, and the dead weight of time regains a lively beat. Unexpected detours add percussion. Hurts add symphony, and each surprise becomes a cymbal of your trust.

Singing your way through retirement may not be possible when something bad or good momentarily takes your breath away. Yet, whatever makes you winded will eventually remind you of God. As you think of His goodness, in strange places or familiar, sing harmonious praises to His unchanging name.

Prayer: Oh, Lord, help my prayers become praises of You in Jesus' name.

Journey with God: Talk with God about an unfamiliar place, situation, or relationship that makes you feel more like complaining than singing. Ask Him to help you recall your reasons to praise Him.

_____

_____

_____

_____

_____

_____

_____

_____

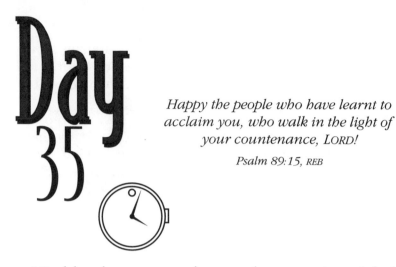

Day 35

Happy the people who have learnt to acclaim you, who walk in the light of your countenance, LORD!

Psalm 89:15, REB

"God has been so good to me, but sometimes I feel like such an ingrate!"

Punishing yourself for occasional displeasure doesn't please God or praise Him. He prefers that you just learn, and that's what praising God is: *acquired* acclamation.

Most people are born crying, not acclaiming. Yet, from womb to tomb, self-centeredness encircles oneself and no one else. That doesn't mean you have no cause for tears. If you don't now, sooner or later, you will! So when you must cry, do; God created an effective cleansing system for that very purpose.

Those teeny tiny tear ducts, however, give a big clue: They're not nearly the dimensions of one's mouth! If you continually let your lips "weep," that can become a hazard to your spiritual health! Usually it's not fatal, but the symptoms show a need to change old habits and become willing to learn the *happiness* of praise. God will help. Just ask Him to make you aware of His goodness, then confine your weeping to times of prayer. If you have to pray forty times a day, so be it, but start and end each tear-time with praise.

As you do this, God beams "the light of His countenance" upon you like a gracious, holy smile—one that gets you smiling again too. Isn't that just like a loving father? Instead of God being self-centered and keeping your praise all to Himself with nothing in it for you, your praise makes God happy with you, and you with Him. He's delighted, you're delighted, and that's how He meant for you to be.

Prayer: Dear Father, thank You for thinking of me! Forgive me for not always learning to acclaim You. Forgive me for bad-mouthing myself, other people, and You with chronic tears or complaints. Happy or sad, help me to walk in the light of Your Word, knowing You speak to each situation I face. Thank You for listening carefully to everything I say. Praise You for encouraging me to praise You in Jesus' name.

Journey with God: Praise God.

_____

_____

_____

_____

_____

_____

_____

_____

_____

Day 36

Let us come into his presence with thanksgiving; let us make a joyful noise to him with songs of praise!

Psalm 95:2, NRSV

Can you sing on key? If so, your church choir might welcome the addition of your fine voice. If not, sing off and away! Every time you stand in a church service with a hymn book opened and ready to use, you become part of God's own choir. Oh, your high notes might scratch the stained glass or your low notes rumble a pew, but you still can do what the Bible asks. You can make a joyful noise!

To warm up to the task, start by giving thanks. Come to church with words and thoughts of thanksgiving. Thank God for your ability to attend the service. Thank Him for those who accompany you or who will soon join you in song.

Thank Him for the music, teachers, pastor, and prayers. Thank Him for providing a sanctuary for His people. Thank Him for immediately bringing you into His presence without keeping you waiting in line to have an audience with Him.

As you thank God for His good gifts, you join His good company, but you also make yourself ready to embrace Him with your praise. Your words and thoughts show your adoration, admiration, and acclamation of who God is, was, and will be forever. So give Him a standing ovation as you sing! Applaud Him with the joyful noise you bring. With a gift of praise, verbalize, vocalize, and harmonize your worship with others who have come to pay tribute to the Almighty King.

Although your praise and thanksgiving are your personal tasks, they don't relieve you from service or retire you from the company of other Christians. With this psalm resounding, say, "Let *us* come into God's presence with thanksgiving. Let *us* make a joyful noise to Him with songs of praise."

Prayer: Heavenly Father, help me to thank and praise You with private and corporate worship worthy of Christ's name.

Journey with God: Does your church attendance attend to your praise and thanksgiving of God? Ask Him to help you know what mars or bars your worship. What's needed to help you worship Him more fully, alone and with other Christians too?

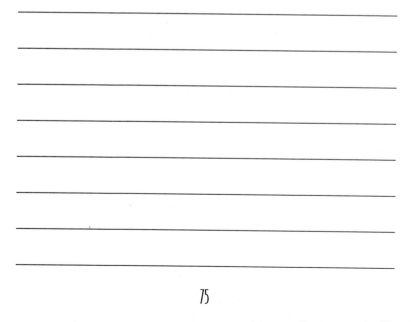

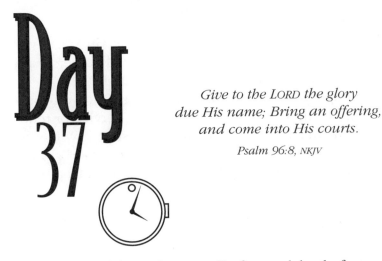

Day 37

*Give to the LORD the glory
due His name; Bring an offering,
and come into His courts.*

Psalm 96:8, NKJV

Were you able to clear up all of your debts before you retired? If so, praise God! You've been blessed with the ability to spend, save, share, and enjoy financial resources. No matter how small your debt or great your fortune, you cannot possibly repay God. His goodness and good gifts far exceed anything you can ever afford!

Fortunately, God still welcomes the gifts of His people. If you're gifted with time, talents, or treasures, you can give from the wealth you've inherited from Him. If you're on a fixed income or an exceptionally tight schedule, your limited reserves may need God's unlimited resources to enable you to bring an offering free of worry or resentment. Rich or poor, you're not expected to give what is not available. Nevertheless, God wants you to make available to Him *all* that you have!

The glory due His name cannot be estimated according to the quantity or even the quality of your possessions, ability, or strength. It doesn't add up to a mere 10 percent of your money, talent, or time. Such a sum would be a levy, duty, surcharge, tariff, toll, or tax; but God's gifts of love are holy tax deductible! He's already paid what He requires. He's already given you what He most desires—you!

The glory due God's name totals 100 percent of all that you have and are. That's quite a price, but with your tithe and offering comes a glorious refund! Through His Holy Spirit, God's interest takes care of you, now and forever. Through His priceless peace offering of Jesus Christ, His lifetime compensation for you extends throughout eternity.

Prayer: Dear Heavenly Father, help me to glorify You with the praise and thanksgiving that is due You for all You've given me in Jesus' holy name.

Journey with God: Ask God what He most wants you to offer to Him. Ask Him to help you clearly know the amount of time and money He wants you to give into the care and service of your church. Thank Him for making up the difference in anything you lack.

_____

_____

_____

_____

_____

_____

_____

_____

Day 38

*O come, let us worship
and bow down, let us kneel
before the LORD, our Maker!*

Psalm 95:6, NRSV

"My arthritis is acting up, so I think I'll skip the church service today."

Retired or not, most people can think of excuses to stay home on a weeknight or Sunday morning, and pain is one of the best reasons! Who can argue with the intensity of discomfort you feel? Who knows what agony it takes for you to get dressed and ready for a worship service? Who knows the amount of effort it takes for you to be in the rain, heat, wind, ice, or snow? Who knows how much chill will stiffen your neck, back, hand, or knee? And who knows how much of a dampened spirit, dreary outlook, or cold attitude will stop you from bowing to God's will and bending to Him in worship?

God knows that some retirees simply cannot get up, even with a walker, wheelchair, or cane. If you happen to be in that condition, however, you can still worship Him. You can still bow to His will from your pillow or bed. You can even bring an offering of your pain. Perhaps He will heal it. Or He might call you to a life of prayer offered from your room.

Regardless of your situation, come. Worship. Bow before God in affection and affliction. If you can't join others in worship, invite them to join you. Whether you participate from a bed rail or an altar rail, you become

Christ's church when two or more gather in His name. So pray together, sing together, and read God's Word together. Bring to Him whatever you have to offer—thousands of dollars or thousands of hours of costly pain invested with Him in prayer.

Prayer: Dear Lord God, I want to worship You, but sometimes I don't know how. Help me, Lord. I choose to bow in submission to Your will as I kneel before You with all I have. Thank You for taking my pressures, problems, and pain and for making my life one with Yours in Jesus' name.

Journey with God: Has anyone ever accused you of being set in your ways? Ask God to reveal to you anything that keeps you from being flexible and pliable—physically, mentally, or spiritually. Discuss what's needed to exchange your ways for His.

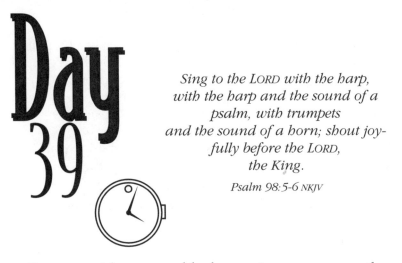

Day 39

Sing to the LORD with the harp, with the harp and the sound of a psalm, with trumpets and the sound of a horn; shout joyfully before the LORD, the King.

Psalm 98:5-6 NKJV

Do you wish you could play a piano or some other musical instrument? Maybe you couldn't take lessons or even practice as long as a career or growing family occupied your time, and now you fear you won't be able to learn. If so, you might welcome some good news: retirees make excellent musicians. In fact, many instructors prefer students in their seventies or those who show mature interest in their lessons.

Actually, age doesn't affect musical aptitude, nor does it affect your ability to draw, to paint, or to write poetry or prose. Either you have it or you don't! If you're attracted to any of those pursuits, however, you probably do have some degree of aptitude or you wouldn't be interested. Also, what may be lacking in natural ability can often be compensated for through the acquisition of technical skill.

If you've always wanted to play a musical instrument, paint, write poetry, or sing in a choir, now is an excellent time to learn. Since you've retired from a salaried position, you're in a better position to concentrate on something new. You're more inclined to occupy your free time with occupations that use your untapped talent or interests. Who knows? Maybe you'll succeed in becoming a published poet or playing in a philharmonic orchestra or gaining an audience for your voice or art, but that's not the point! The goal is to sound the talent that's found. As you delight in the discovery, training, and use of God's good gifts, you show real aptitude for *shouting joyfully* before the Lord.

Prayer: Dear Heavenly Father, thank You for the interests and inclinations You've given me. Help me to train and use them for Your glory in Christ's name.

Journey with God: If you've denied or ignored a God-given talent or ability, ask God to reveal what is keeping you from pursuing that interest now. Talk with Him about ways to renew your enthusiasm, thereby enabling you to shout with joy.

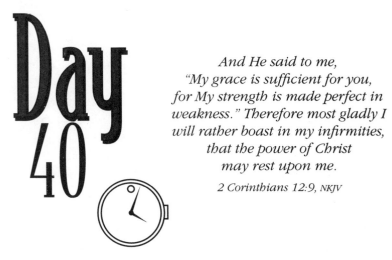

And He said to me,
"My grace is sufficient for you,
for My strength is made perfect in
weakness." Therefore most gladly I
will rather boast in my infirmities,
that the power of Christ
may rest upon me.

2 Corinthians 12:9, NKJV

"There's nothing I'd like better than to _____, but I just can't do it right now because _____."

Having a special aptitude or interest doesn't mean you can easily pursue it. Perhaps you're physically disabled and can't enroll in a class you'd like to take. Or maybe you're in a financial bind and don't have the money for lessons and materials. Maybe you fear getting out by yourself or being in the company of other people. Maybe you feel so discouraged by someone's negative comments, manipulation, or control that you're confused about what you even want. Maybe you're too weak with worry to try anything new.

Weakness comes in many forms but often shows itself in a physical, mental, or financial condition. Debilitation of some kind can happen to anyone—and usually does! Sooner or later, most people suffer from at least one area of weakness; if you haven't, that's too bad! It's one of those paradoxes found in the spiritual realm: when you're the strongest, that's when you're apt to be more in need of God.

Conversely, any speck or spot of deficiency reveals the area in which you'll be quickest to seek God's help and strength. So if you're weak and you know it, go ahead and show it! Pray for help. When you get it, praise the Lord.

Prayer: Dear God, I don't like to admit a weakness to myself, much less to You or anyone else! Forgive my pride in even thinking that I'm just fine without You! I need You, Lord.

Help me to know what I want. Help me to discover my abilities and strengths. But more than that, help me to learn of Your almighty power that is available to me in Jesus' name.

Journey with God: In this space, ask God to guide you in filling in the blanks about what you want to do, learn, or try. Ask Him to fill in the gaps that hinder you from moving toward your special interests. Look for Him to provide His strength and solutions for each of those areas.

_____

_____

_____

_____

_____

_____

_____

_____

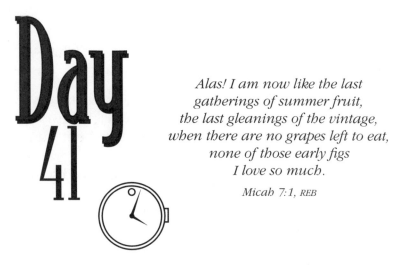

Day 41

*Alas! I am now like the last
gatherings of summer fruit,
the last gleanings of the vintage,
when there are no grapes left to eat,
none of those early figs
I love so much.*

Micah 7:1, REB

Have you lost your appetite? Physical illness usually decreases a desire for food until nothing tastes particularly good. Sometimes medications can alter taste buds or make formerly favorite foods suddenly seem tasteless. If you dread the daily chore of eating alone, that can make mealtimes unappetizing too. Maybe you're just tired of cooking! Yet, retirees who don't have contact with other people may be so starved for companionship that they will try to feed that hunger with anything their refrigerator holds.

In feast or famine, physical strength fluctuates with the amount and types of foods consumed. If you generally eat three well-balanced meals a day, you probably have no cause for concern. Perhaps you already place fresh fruit, whole grains, and raw vegetables high on your grocery list. Yet if you often eat junk food or no food, you may be too tired to go anywhere or do much of anything.

God created your body and gave it to you to maintain. He never said, "Here, this bulk (or bag of bones) is your problem now!" Instead, He provided everything that is needed for you to take good care of yourself. Hopefully, you're doing just that. If not, talk with Him about your diet. Ask Him to help you learn more about the specific foods or food supplements that supply or deplete your physical strength. Don't be concerned about fads but about sources of nutrition for your body. Ask God to help you know what you need. Then don't be surprised if the best foods for you are the very ones that sound good or that keep coming to your mind.

Prayer: Dear God, I hear so much talk about no-fat, no-salt, no-sugar foods; it makes me think there's nothing good for me that tastes good! Help me, Lord, to hear what You say and to know what I need to stay strong in Jesus' name.

Journey with God: Do you feel like a dried-up grape or a fat fig? If a loved one ate what you do, would you want him or her to change diets? Talk with God about your eating habits.

_____

_____

_____

_____

_____

_____

_____

_____

Day 42

*Through your favour
we hold our heads high.*

Psalm 89:17b, REB

In the first weeks of retirement, people who seldom get sick might suddenly find themselves feeling lousy! If that's happened to you, the condition might not be due to a physical weakness so much as to a mental or emotional struggle. Perhaps you're unsure what to do with yourself and just don't feel like getting out of bed. Maybe you pursued a new relationship or area of interest that didn't work out as you had hoped.

Physical weakness sometimes indicates a need for physical change such as adding more exercise or practicing better nutrition. Similarly, mental fatigue can show a weakened mind-set that also needs to be corrected. How? The direction for that change may start at chin level! Usually its *altitude* shows *attitude*. For example, if you throw your head back proudly, your face most notably features nostrils. If you carry a low-level chin, you might drop your outlook until you grate your nerves on a sidewalk.

To be in sound mind and have emotional strength, here's the biblical position:

1. *Confess!* Don't rely on your own mental outlook, brilliance, or perfection, but on strength and power from God.

2. *Accept and believe.* You're human; God isn't. Only His favor brings you the forgiveness you need to counterbalance every sin, failure, and stupidity, whether real or imagined.

3. *Stand.* Through Christ, get your mind, your past, and your shoulders squared with God's righteousness, not your own.

4. *Walk in His Spirit.* With His guidance, you're able to walk upright without looking down on yourself or anyone else.

5. *Hold your head high.* This position comes as you recognize your own disabilities and look not to yourself or to other people, but *up to God.* In Him comes your confidence and strength.

Prayer: Thank You, Lord, for putting me right with You and keeping me in the favor of Jesus' name.

Journey with God: Ask God to show where you're missing a step in gaining the mental and emotional well-being that He has in mind for you.

_____

_____

_____

_____

_____

_____

_____

Day 43

But I shall watch for the LORD,
I shall wait for God my saviour;
my God will hear me.

Micah 7:7, REB

Don't you sometimes get tired of waiting? Waiting for the phone to ring . . . for a pension check to come . . . for a doctor's report . . . in line at the grocery store . . . for physical or mental fatigue to go away. . . to feel good again.

If you disliked your former job, you probably felt as though you had to wait a long time for this day of retirement to arrive. Yet, it did! Most likely, other long-awaited times will come too, but sometimes the delays seem hard to bear. Right now, for instance, you may be waiting to hear the outcome of someone's surgery or whether you'll need to have an operation yourself. If you have grown children, you might be waiting for them to invite you for a visit or to invite Christ into their lives.

Some long-awaited moments concern your physical well-being. Others involve your mental outlook or emotional good health. Yet, no matter what you await—or what awaits you—God patiently longs for you to seek Him. He waits for you to come to Him with every problem that arises, but He also awaits your calls and requests anytime of the day or night. He anticipates your reports of thanksgiving and praise. Even more, however, He awaits *His operation* of your life.

In crisis and conflict, in good times and bad, in long delays and spontaneous outbursts, God longs to have you with Him. He wants you to talk with Him, having the assurance that He will always listen and respond. He wants you to wait for Him to take the lead. He wants you to trust His love and timing more and more as you get to know Him well. So what are you waiting for? With eager anticipation, await your Lord and Savior. Right on time, as always, He'll be there.

Prayer: Heavenly Father, please help me to keep each waiting room open to You in Jesus' name.

Journey with God: In what areas do you expect God to be there, waiting with you? In what ways does He want you to wait up for Him?

_____

_____

_____

_____

_____

_____

_____

_____

_____

_____

Day 44

*"Indeed these are the mere edges of
His ways, And how small a whisper
we hear of Him! But the thunder of
His power who can understand?"*

Job 26:14, NKJV

As your primary occupation becomes occupying
yourself more and more with God, you may wonder
how you'll know what He's saying to you. Trying to hear
Him can be frustrating at times, especially if another
Christian seems to tune in well enough to state, "The
Lord told me you should." Unless God has reason to
broadcast an announcement, you'll usually hear His personal instruction to you before anyone else does—
assuming, of course, that you're listening. Even then,
you won't often hear with an ear!

Each time you read the Bible, God reveals Himself to
you. As you let His Holy Spirit occupy and instruct you,
the Bible suddenly becomes alive. It becomes a personal
letter—a whole Book written just for you! The promises
of God have your name on them. Biblical prayers become your own as you claim and personalize them with
names of family members, friends, or foes to whom they
apply.

During your devotional time, you'll "hear" God speak
as He brings a clear insight, inspiration, idea, or impres-
sion to your mind. If your own thoughts distract you,
just ask God to quiet them so you can hear Him well.
Then trust that He will. He wants to communicate with
you. After all, He gave you His Word and His Son! The

Bible also promises that God will give His Holy Spirit and holy thoughts to those who ask.

As assurance, you'll have an inner knowing or peace when you hear God's voice within. Often, circumstances also will help to clarify His personal word or plan for you. So listen. God might not answer every question or reveal everything at once, but His whisper will come. You'll hear Him speak of His ways as His loving thoughts quietly edge into your mind.

Prayer: Oh, Lord, fill me with Your Holy Spirit and Your Word in Jesus' name.

Journey with God: Ask God to edge out every distraction and even the slightest fringe of disruption as you come to Him during this journaling time. Note and write what you hear.

Day 45

"Since times are not hidden
from the Almighty,
Why do those who know Him
see not His days?"

Job 24:1, NKJV

"What's happening?"
"I have no idea!"

As you spend time becoming more acquainted with God, you might wonder, *What's He doing?* No matter how well you know Him, everything God says or does won't always make sense! If you sought Him in days past and seek Him in times ahead, however, you might as well trust Him right now!

Nothing is hidden from God. He sees a panoramic yet microscopic view of you and your life. He knows that some days are better for you than others, as they bring more pleasure than pain and more joy than sorrow. To God, though, every day has equal value. Everyday He's there. Everyday He puts in time with you, occupying Himself with each concern, each need, each desire.

As God continues His work of *perfecting* you, He knows what's needed for you to be *perfectly* yourself. He knows what it would take for you to live happily ever after as the person He created. He knows who you are and what work He has yet to do. So, of course, He wants you to cooperate, obey, and express interest! God wants your attention every day. He wants your willingness to see Him in all things and your faith to know that "God is at work," despite contrary appearances or pain.

Some days, you'll feel like saying, "Ouch!" Other days, "Wow!" Don't worry; God expects both! Either way, thank Him. Be glad that your fears or discomforts aren't hidden from Him. Be quick to listen, quick to see. Each day, show your joy and appreciation for all He's doing—even if you have absolutely no idea what that is!

Prayer: Heavenly Father, thank You for being with me in all times and places. Help me to see Your hand at work. When I can't, help me to trust that You're always here in Jesus' name.

Journey with God: Have you thanked God for all He's done for you in the past? Can you see Him at work or trust that He's with you in a difficult situation now? What do you have to say for God's good work in you? Talk with Him about any response other than, "Thanks!"

_____

_____

_____

_____

_____

_____

_____

_____

Day 46

*The Son of God was revealed
for this purpose,
to destroy the works
of the devil.*

1 John 3:8b, NRSV

To know God is to know good. Unfortunately, some think that's not good enough! They see so much violence that they ask, "Why does a loving God allow such things?" Asking *why,* however, could bring fewer answers and less understanding of God's character than asking *what* or *how.* For example, you might ask, "How can evil be judged *before* God's judgment comes?"

In criminal courts around this country, a judge has the power to deny bail and keep a potentially dangerous criminal in custody for the duration of a trial. Although no sentence has been carried out, the person is temporarily locked up and kept from committing more crimes. Similarly, God uses interim means. He's already provided the Way to keep evil in check.

He's already reversed the verdict against mankind as His Word in Christ turned the word *evil* backward and made it *l-i-v-e!*

Because He's merciful, God wants all to live and none to perish. He wants everyone to have the opportunity to repent before He comes again. Until then, God cannot condone evil or injustice. He Himself is good and just. Therefore He sent His Holy Spirit until the trials end and the final day of judgment comes. As "bodyguard" for the church, the Holy Spirit watches over God's people and empowers them to triumph: good over evil. So, as you believe and pray in Jesus' name, you make a citizen's arrest! You place yourself in safekeeping and dark powers into the custody of your Lord and Savior Jesus Christ.

Prayer: Holy Father, forgive me for demanding explanations or putting You on trial! Forgive me for not always believing that Your power exceeds anything in heaven or on earth. Help me to attest to Your strength and goodness. Thank You for empowering me with Your Holy Spirit and guiding me into Your ongoing work of prayer in Jesus' name.

Journey with God: Jesus said His followers would "do greater works"—i.e., His Holy Spirit would dwell in them wherever they lived—not just in Jerusalem, but around the world. As you see terrible things happening in your part of that world, ask God how He wants you to pray for each situation.

_____

_____

_____

_____

_____

_____

_____

*"Believe Me
that I am in the Father
and the Father in Me,
or else believe Me for the sake
of the works themselves."*

John 14:11, NKJV

"Did I show you the latest pictures of my grandchild?" Maybe you have photos of another family member or friend scattered around your house. Such reminders can make a person seem closer to you, but they also give you an opportunity to show your favorite people or loved ones to someone else.

What picture do you present of God? Do you carry around a quick snapshot of His work—one that doesn't look very much like Him? Do you still have an unflattering portrait you sketchily drew in childhood—a picture that represents an immature view of God drawn from scary stories or a blurred Old Testament figure that you couldn't see too well?

Getting a good likeness of God isn't easy for adults, much less children! Even now, you will not want to retire yourself into His care if you think of Him as mean! Perhaps you had Him confused with a crotchety adult or older relative who treated you badly. Maybe you feared Him with the terror you had for the bogeyman—something frightening, mysterious, and unknown. Maybe you need to revise or erase an old view.

To get a more accurate picture of God, look at His Son. Read the Gospels and see the "family resemblance" in the actions taken and the words spoken by Christ. See how Jesus communicated with people—how He loved, taught, chastised, fed, healed, and forgave. See what moved Him to tears or to laughter. See how He prayed. See His power. Then you'll see God, and you'll also see some resemblance of Him in yourself.

Prayer: Dear Father God, I don't always like the picture I have of You or myself. Please show me a new view as I read Your Word. Reveal Yourself to me through Your Holy Spirit and draw me to a closer look at You in Jesus' name.

Journey with God: Is your view of God an old picture from childhood? Do you have frequent exposure to what He's truly like? Who is this God you follow? In what ways do you closely resemble Him?

_____

_____

_____

_____

_____

_____

_____

_____

_____

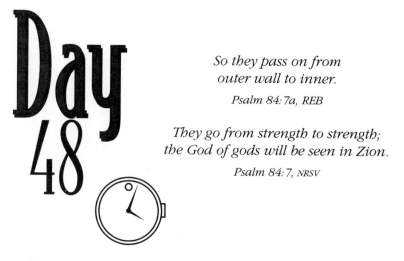

*So they pass on from
outer wall to inner.*

Psalm 84:7a, REB

*They go from strength to strength;
the God of gods will be seen in Zion.*

Psalm 84:7, NRSV

For years, you went to work regularly, even if your office happened to be at home. Hopefully, you enjoyed doing whatever was required of you, but whether or not you liked the work, your job remained outside yourself. If you didn't feel too well, you could either stay home to regain strength or push aside tasks for the rest of the day. Now all of that's changed.

Instead of an outside job, you have an inner work going on. This occupation requires mental, physical, and spiritual stamina, but not from you—from God. Sometimes such strength might be hard to detect because it usually doesn't come through outer appearances or ability. God works on your spirit from the inside out. Through the power of His Son, His Word, and His Holy Spirit, God gives you inner strength that you didn't know you had! Apart from God, you *don't* have it. You just don't have the spiritual vigor that life rigorously requires.

As you enter more fully into retirement from the working world, you go from the outer work of yourself to God's inner workings. He becomes your energy and power for all you need.

He helps you to look upward instead of inward to yourself. He especially wants you to look toward Him instead of outward to other people. If this makes you feel oddly out of control, praise God for letting you know you are! He is in charge and fully in command of His work in you.

Often, this secret of "power in powerlessness" escapes those who rush off to work, thinking they can take care of everything themselves. Unaware of their limitations or need for God, they go in their own strength—from weakness to weakness. As you reverse that, you might feel more and more helpless, but you'll be more and more helped! The God of gods will be seen inside out as He passes on His strength to you.

Prayer: Thank You, Lord, for showing Your power and glory to me in Jesus' name.

Journey with God: In what ways do you feel powerless to effect changes in your self, home, church, or community? Ask God to reveal to you His will and His work in those areas.

_____

_____

_____

_____

_____

_____

_____

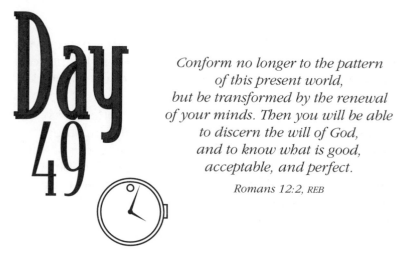

Day 49

*Conform no longer to the pattern
of this present world,
but be transformed by the renewal
of your minds. Then you will be able
to discern the will of God,
and to know what is good,
acceptable, and perfect.*

Romans 12:2, REB

"Wow, what a transformation! You look great! Retirement certainly does agree with you."

If you came out of an extremely stressful job situation, you might look like you've just had a makeover! In a way, you have. Instead of making over a client, project, or boss, you've made up your mind to follow God. That decision changes how you look at everything—and how everyone looks at you!

To get along in the job world, you probably conformed at times to its pattern. Perhaps you rushed through traffic or toward deadlines. Maybe you were shaped by subtle demands to perform or by a high-pressure environment working to conform you to itself. During retirement, however, you no longer have to perform or conform. You don't have to get misshapen by other people's expectations until you feel deformed in soul or spirit. You don't have to reform either! Now you can be *transformed*—not by congregations, clients, customers, co-workers, employers, employees, partners, principals, students, or your own efforts—but by God Himself.

To *be* transformed requires a different mind-set than that of the working world. Your decision to follow God begins this transformation as you put thought and energy into hearing and obeying Him. This becomes your goal and endeavor while God's work provides the actual power to transform. He *converts* your thoughts and energy. As your will converges with His, you're then able to discern what He wants. Your daily pattern will be set to know what is good, acceptable, and perfect to Him.

Prayer: Heavenly Father, sometimes I think I've spent my life trying to please other people or myself. Even when I didn't know what was expected, I still tried! I never meant to be a conformist, but worldly patterns are so clear to see. Turn me around, Lord, so I can clearly discern Your will and ways. Help me to be converted by You into the person You want me to be. Thank You for making me good, acceptable, and perfect in the transforming power of Jesus' name.

Journey with God: In what way is God converting you?

_____

_____

_____

_____

_____

_____

_____

_____

Day 50

Beloved, now we are children of God; and it has not yet been revealed what we shall be, but we know that when He is revealed, we shall be like Him, for we shall see Him as He is.

1 John 3:2, NKJV

Did someone you know recently pass away? Do you have some concerns about your own health? Are you afraid to get out, travel, or fly? Are you afraid to die? If so, don't *be* afraid; *be* loved. Regardless of age, that's what you are: God's own *be*-loved child.

Now that you've retired, maybe you don't feel like a kid anymore. Maybe retirement made you age so fast that you've already shopped for a cemetery plot, talked to your church about the service you want, and made sure the organist keeps playing through the last stanza of "Amazing Grace." If so, great! By purchasing a grave-site and making funeral arrangements now, you'll keep your family from having to deal with the stress of those decisions during a time of grief. You also have the advantage of selecting a pleasant place for people to gather in your honor although you probably won't be there yourself!

No one knows exactly what death is like or how long it takes to get there. However, the Bible assures you that, when you find out, you won't be afraid. You'll be like Him. You'll see God as He is, and you'll just want to *be* more of that likeness than you have ever been. You won't be lost. You'll be found, and isn't that just like love? God finds and heals His family into a loving relationship with Himself. So don't be afraid. Be loved. God knows right where to find you: in His love for you and yours for Him.

Prayer: Heavenly Father, I guess I'm more afraid of dying than I want to admit. I especially don't like the thought of losing people I love. O Lord, let me lose no one! Help my family and friends find Your eternal love in the salvation of Christ's name. Help me always to be in love with You.

Journey with God: What unknowns do you fear? What prior arrangements does God want you to make concerning death? Pray for Christ's salvation and Holy Spirit to come into each person that God brings to your mind.

_____

_____

_____

_____

_____

_____

_____

_____

_____

Day 51

*I have been crucified with Christ: the
life I now live is not my life, but the
life which Christ lives in me; and my
present mortal life is lived by faith in
the Son of God, who loved me and
gave himself up for me.*

Galatians 2:20, REB

"Where there's a will, there's a way." That old adage
doesn't always stand up in court, so it may be more accurate to say, "Where there's a will, there's a way to
break it!"

Since a living trust can't be contested as easily as a
will, you might talk with your attorney and your financial planner about making those arrangements. A living
trust can bring you the assurance that your financial
wishes will be carried out while you're still alive and
after your death too. By making those decisions, you
arrange for distribution of your estate—cash, property,
and other investments—according to your wishes. If
those plans change, you'll be able to alter your living
trust, but no one else can.

A living will includes none of this. Instead of making
arrangements for your estate, a living will assures that in
a medical situation, your desires will bc carried out
should a life-or-death decision arise. By signing this doc-
ument, you let family and physicians know where you
draw the line. With a living will, you can say, "No way
do I want to be kept alive artificially!"

Do you want to be kept alive spiritually? Do you
know without a doubt that you will live forever with
God? Because of His "living will," Christ Jesus dwells

within you—now and throughout eternity. You can contest His will, or you can let your life be carried out according to His wishes. So live in living trust of Him. Be assured that His Holy Spirit signs and seals His unbreakable will: Christ's life lived in you.

Prayer: Dear Lord, all this talk about prior arrangements makes me uncomfortable. I don't even want to think about dying, much less plan for it! Help me to hear and make decisions that please You. Praise You for the life-giving provision of Your Holy Spirit within me in Jesus' name.

Journey with God: Ask God how He wants to carry out His plans in your daily life. In what ways have you contested His will?

_____

_____

_____

_____

_____

_____

_____

_____

_____

Day 52

So teach us to number our days,
That we may gain a heart of wisdom.

Psalm 90:12, NKJV

My days are numbered.

Actually, they always were. But now that you've retired, you may suddenly be more aware of that! Such time constraints might urge you to make arrangements for death, and that's a good idea. Your family will be spared from having to make difficult decisions or attempting to guess what you would've wanted had you taken the time yourself to say! Meanwhile, you're very much alive, so wisely use the time you have.

In the first weeks of retirement, you might be tempted to try everything you ever wanted to try and do everything you ever wanted to do! Most likely, you'll find excellent opportunities available. For example, if you moved into a retirement community or an area known for its number of retirees, you'll discover all sorts of activities aimed at your special interests. Colleges design courses for adult education. Job fairs and volunteer groups entice mature workers. Community Centers focus activities around senior citizens. The YMCA and YWCA sponsor classes, such as low-impact aerobics or high-impact tips for your decor.

Although it's tempting to hurry up and try everything, be wise about your use of time. Before you sign up for any class or commitment, seek God first. Let Him lead you into activities that are just right for you. Let your first action be ongoing prayer times devoted to hearing and following Him.

Prayer: Dear God, You've got my number! Thank You for calling on me to count each day worthy of You. Help me to make You first in my life. Help me to hear Your choice for me *before* I make arrangements or commitments to pursue new activities. Help me to value each moment You've given me to live fully in the wisdom of Christ's name.

Journey with God: Do you sometimes feel like you're wasting away? Do you ever wish you'd just go ahead and die? Quick! Ask God to help you die immediately to self-centeredness and self-will, including worrying about other people's will for you. Ask Him to help you use time wisely and to place His full value on your days without number!

_____

_____

_____

_____

_____

_____

_____

_____

Day 53

I will lie down and sleep in peace,
for you alone, O LORD,
make me dwell in safety.

Psalm 4:8, NIV

Oh, I wish everybody would just let me be! To join or not to join social activities is your choice, no one else's. Only you can be you. Only you can let yourself be. So, how *be* you? Are you learning to be at rest? Are you relaxing and enjoying this time of being retired?

To be or not to be the person God created you to be is a question you face each day. Hopefully, you're discovering answers about yourself and God's will as you continue your daily devotions. By reading the Bible, praying, and listening, you have a better idea of what God wants you to do. Before you *do* anything though, become spiritually awake to your resting place in God. Dwell safely as the person He wants you to *be.*

Who are you anyway? Part of you has been shaped by genetics, experiences, and environment. Another part you shape yourself by choices and actions, but also by your *reactions* to what you have received. For instance, if you usually have an adverse reaction to each challenge or change you face, your countenance or responses might be negative. If you're quick to see God in every new situation—or at least suspect He's at work—you may be a person of great faith.

Who you are depends on many factors, some of which you can control, and some you can't. The person you're to become, however, begins with belief! Your belief in God and His goodness helps to shape your unique, individual character. Yet His Word reveals the Beatitudes He wants for all of His children. Only by knowing what God thinks and wants can you be better behaved as His beloved child. Only by knowing who He is can you begin to see who your Lord meant you to be.

Prayer: Dear Father, help me to be at peace with You and to know Your mind and attitudes for me. Help me to live in the safety of who I am in You in Jesus' name.

Journey with God: When you were growing up, did you memorize the Beatitudes? Do you need to refresh your memory now? Ask God to help you recite His attitudes about yourself and your relationships with other people. Pray for your thoughts and actions to be at rest in Christ.

_____

_____

_____

_____

_____

_____

_____

_____

_____

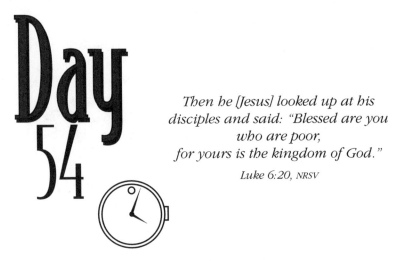

Day 54

*Then he [Jesus] looked up at his
disciples and said: "Blessed are you
who are poor,
for yours is the kingdom of God."*

Luke 6:20, NRSV

If your retirement years have been blessed with money, you probably don't like to hear Jesus' Beatitude about being poor! Remember, though, that He did not suggest that you strive to be insolvent or beg to be broke! Christ never said, "If you're wealthy, you'd better feel guilty about it!"

God's Word consistently shows that every good gift comes from Him, including the possession and enjoyment of financial means. Yet Christians often seem to think they're supposed to prefer poverty over riches. Matthew 5:3 clarifies Christ's attitude: "Blessed are the poor in spirit, for theirs is the kingdom of heaven" (NRSV).

If you have a limited or fixed income, you have the advantage of *knowing* you need help! If not, don't be eager to be meager, but hurry and ask God to reveal the impoverishment you have apart from Him. Give Him credit for His good gifts. Be thankful. Be always aware of your spiritual need. Don't think so much about what you do or don't have that you pay poor attention to God!

The more you understand this, the more you may wonder why so many Christians don't get it! Today's verse clarifies that too. It says, "He (Jesus) looked at His disciples." They were the people who followed Him closely. They were the ones who had left everything to be in His company. They were the followers who had retired from their own wealth, ways, and work so they could sit at Jesus' feet. As you also sit in silence, listening, you learn about being His disciple. You follow Christ into His kingdom—that blessed and perfect place to be in the presence and power of God.

Prayer: Dear God, I can't imagine life without You! When I'm not close to You, I feel so destitute. Help me always to be aware of my emptiness without You. Help me to be filled with Your Spirit so I can live abundantly for You in Jesus' name.

Journey with God: Wealthy or not, do you consider money more valuable than God? In what ways do you feel impoverished?

_____

_____

_____

_____

_____

_____

_____

_____

Day 55

*"Blessed are those who mourn,
For they shall be comforted."*

Matthew 5:4, NKJV

It's no use. I can't do anything like I once could! That's probably not entirely true, yet your feelings are certainly real. So what makes you feel like wailing? Do you lament lost love, youth, health, work, or opportunities? What brings your tears to God's ears? Be specific as you consider: *Can I do something about this? Can God?*

If you're filled with remorse, regret, or unrest, you need to exchange that for forgiveness. If you're infused with confusion, uncertainty, or insecurity, you need to be filled with secure faith and hope. If you're empty of energy and strength, you need to be filled with power. If you're lonely, pained, grieved, disquieted, dismayed, or disconcerted, you need to be filled with comfort. You can buoy yourself with positive thoughts or wishful thinking, but they won't replace or complete what's there. *To be filled you need God.*

God's Word promises forgiveness—something that's only His to give. God's Word secures your faith and hope in Him. God's Word empowers you with His wisdom. God's Word speaks directly to you, no matter what causes you to mourn. God's Word presents to you His Son, Christ Jesus.

According to God's Word made flesh, Jesus promised that your mourning would cease. He acknowledged your need, knowing full well the painful work He would do. Facing the agony of the cross, He gave His Word to comfort you. With resurrection power, He provided the Holy Comforter. God knew that only He could ease your pain. He knows the full measure of emptiness it costs you to be filled.

Prayer: Dear Lord, how great Your sacrifice! How strong Your power! Praise You for the holy comfort of Christ's name.

Journey with God: Have you received the ultimate comfort of God's forgiveness? Have you accepted Jesus Christ as your only possible Savior—the One who comforts God from ever having to mourn His loss of you? Have you been filled with the Holy Comforter sent to you in Jesus' name? Pray for the light of God's Word to dawn in each new mourning.

_____

_____

_____

_____

_____

_____

_____

Day 56

"Blessed are the gentle;
they shall have the earth
for their possession."

Matthew 5:5, REB

The first time a younger person called you "Sir" or "Ma'am" did it make you feel old? If someone referred to you as "Such a gentleman!" or "Quite a lady," how would you respond? Would you say something like, "I wish!" or would you acknowledge, at least to yourself, the person's wisdom in recognizing who you are? Well, guess what? You are such a gentlewoman! You are quite a gentleman! How can anyone who doesn't know you be so sure? Simple! You're in the family of the Lord Jesus Christ.

To be gentle implies a noble birth. Man or woman, your nobility comes through your inheritance—either you're *born* into it or you're not. You weren't nobility until Jesus bore you into His Father's presence. As He arose from death on the cross, He carried you into adoption by His Holy Spirit so you could receive the birthright that was due Him. In the nobility of Christ's name and character, you inherit His estate!

Some people think that's not necessary. They think the nobility of mankind or human nature should muster strength to possess the earth and set all things right again. They work hard to obtain goodness through their own efforts. They enact very good laws to promote environmental control or peace among nations. They really want to take care of the earth and leave a safe inheritance for their children. The problem is, the earth isn't theirs to give. In Christ, it's yours!

In the nobility of Christ, you own the world! With ownership comes not only rights and privileges but obligations too. You have the spiritual birthright but also the responsibility to inherit, help, protect, possess, and pray for God to give the whole earth what's due—the gentle but powerful name and blessing of its only Lord and Savior, Jesus Christ.

Prayer: Come, Lord Jesus.

Journey with God: To be blessed as a true gentle man or woman requires submission to God. Submit to Him your thoughts about the earth. Listen to God's response as He shows you what is to be your area of concern.

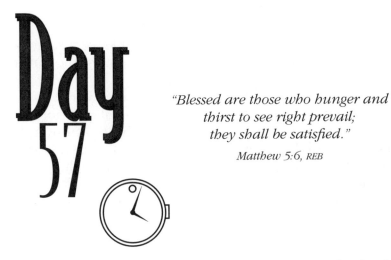

Day 57

*"Blessed are those who hunger and
thirst to see right prevail;
they shall be satisfied."*

Matthew 5:6, REB

"But that's just not right! Why doesn't somebody do something about it?"

Since you're now retired, you probably grew up in a generation other than the one presently at work. With each new era, you witnessed new growth or change. Sometimes that's great, but sometimes it isn't! The difference between the two shows itself as prevailing trends either favor what is right or what is not.

Often, a line cannot be drawn finely between right and wrong, good and bad, or night and day. Even the keenest eye can seldom judge the exact moment of dusk or dawn,. and yet Christians still try, thinking that it's their duty! Christ's Word, however, reveals something quite different. His Beatitude on righteousness does not encourage people to notice the crack in a plate! Instead, He spoke of daily hunger, daily thirst.

When someone asks if you're hungry or if you want something to drink, you might not know. That too can be a very thin line unless you're parched or starved! Then you know for sure, Yes! "Eating is right for me, now!" Or, "Yes, please give me something to drink right this minute!" The immediate need becomes obvious and right. There's no question about it. There's no nit-picking on the plate.

As you see growth and changes in your community or the world, you'll spot obvious things that need to be set right, right away. If there's something you can do to help, first pray! God's attitude is that *you* cannot appease insatiable appetites or ease world hunger, but *He* can satisfy every need. So talk to Him about what's wrong. Set it right before Him in prayer. Then listen. Perhaps He'll remind you He's in charge. Perhaps He will ask you to be involved in filling a need as you offer a cup of water in Christ's name.

Prayer: Holy Father, You alone are judge. You alone can set wrongs right. Help me to remember this in Jesus' name.

Journey with God: To be satisfied yourself as you wait for God to make things right, place obvious wrongs right before Him now in prayer.

_____

_____

_____

_____

_____

_____

_____

_____

Day 58

"Blessed are those who show mercy; mercy shall be shown to them."

Matthew 5:7, REB

"Lord, have mercy!"

You wouldn't even bother to set troubling thirsts and hungers before God in prayer if you didn't know that He does indeed have mercy. He's shown it to you every time you've received forgiveness. You've also obtained some measure of mercy through similar gifts, such as benevolence, tolerance, compassion, empathy, or consideration. As you're endowed with these gifts, you realize that they weren't meant to be hoarded or cast off, but instead passed on to those with whom you have contact.

So how merciful are you? To truly be blessed with mercy, you need a merciful attitude yourself. If you're like most Christians, you have a sense of benevolence as you give to the poor or less fortunate. You show compassion toward other cultures, children, or peoples unlike yourself. You abhor prejudice, violence, infidelity, and abuse, but try to be considerate of those with whom you've worked and worshiped.

Again and again throughout your life, you have surely shown mercy to a spouse, sibling, parent, child, grandchild, friend, neighbor, coworker, or total stranger. Otherwise, if someone stepped on your toes, justice would require you to be a heel to that foot! Instead, mercy allows people to walk away, undeservedly perhaps, but with no discernible limp!

Is that how you've been treated? What measure of mercy do you know and show? Do you stomp on yourself, again and again, for your sins, mistakes, faults, trespasses, and debts?

Do you crush Christ by making His forgiveness invalid? Or do you walk away, forgiven and filled with joy at the mercy you've been shown?

Prayer: Dear Lord, please forgive me for not forgiving myself! Help me to be merciful to myself and others in Christ's name.

Journey with God: Ask God to reveal a time when you've chosen not to receive forgiveness yourself or not to be merciful to someone else. Then for mercy's sake, receive! Give what you have been given to those God brings now to your mind.

_____

_____

_____

_____

_____

_____

_____

Day 59

*"Blessed are those whose
hearts are pure;
they shall see God."*

Matthew 5:8, REB

"If I do that, what's in it for me?"

Worldly people seek this information before making a commitment, but Christians aren't sure if it's OK to ask! Before you consider taking another job or becoming involved in a new activity, you need to assess what you'll get out of it. For instance, maybe you'll realize that you weren't yet ready to retire. Maybe you'll see that you have more to offer in an old area of interest. Maybe you'll learn something new or be ready to develop some part of yourself more fully.

To be pure in heart, you need to know what's in your heart! You need to acknowledge your wants and desires to be able to enjoy life, develop talents, and also keep yourself purely free of resentment! Perhaps you'll discover interests you didn't know you had. Maybe, instead, you'll notice an ulterior motive or selfish purpose that you'd rather not acknowledge.

To be pure in heart requires courage and confession. If you want something, take heart and admit it! If you don't like what you see, muster courage and admit that. Regardless, as you look inside, be truthful. Are you *contented* with the *contents* of your heart? If so, thank God. If not, pray about it, but don't perform heart surgery on yourself!

In your innermost being, you'll find some things you didn't know were there. Some might upset you. Others might bring joyous discoveries about yourself. Either way, to be pure in heart, come clean! Let God remove the impurities He sees. Withhold nothing. Trust His ability to cleanse you. As you see your motives and desires perfected with forgiveness, you'll see more clearly the pure and powerful love of God.

Prayer: Heavenly Father, thank You for the perfect purity of Your love. I like to think I have only flawless motives and innocent purposes or desires, but You know better! Help me to be pure in heart in the cleansing power of Jesus' name.

Journey with God: What are you trying to hide? Whether you think you want something good or bad, fess up! God already knows, but tell Him anyway!

_____

_____

_____

_____

_____

_____

_____

_____

Day 60

"Blessed are the peacemakers,
for they will be called
children of God."

Matthew 5:9, NRSV

"Hey, you started it, not me!"

Would you like to enjoy some "peace and quiet" in your retirement environment? Are you willing to pay any price? The cost isn't blame or resignation! Actively, you become the one to start peacemaking by making peace, not pretense. At the first sign of unfriendly fire you don't hide in a foxhole! You have such a strong commitment to peace that you act on your convictions and say what's on your mind and spirit. You listen to the other side too, as you communicate and resolve the differences that contribute to an atmosphere of war.

To help you see your motives or those of someone else, James 4:1-3 (NRSV) says, "Those conflicts and disputes among you, where do they come from? Do they not come from your cravings that are at war within you?" (The first threat to peace may be the war within yourself!) "You want something and do not have it; so you commit murder." (That's definitely overkill!) "And you covet something and cannot obtain it; so you engage in disputes and conflicts." (A clash of wills, perhaps?) "You do not have because you do not ask." (Hmm . . .) Do you always ask for what you want? Do you acknowledge equally the requests of other people in your home, family, church, or neighborhood? Divorce wars, custody battles, family feuds, church rifts, and world war might be averted if both parties would simply state their case and clearly ask for what they want or need! To be peacemakers, true children of God first listen to what He has to say. They're the ones who start the peace by saying, "Let's stop arguing and start praying about this right now!"

Prayer: Dear Lord, help me to be a true peacemaker as I bring to You each conflict in Christ's name.

Journey with God: If you've committed treason without reason, admit now what you really think! Start by telling God. Listen to His word of acknowledgment and forgiveness. Pray to be a peacemaker in each good fight of faith by asking, "Lord, is my will in conflict with Yours?"

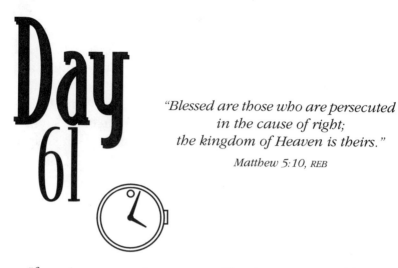

Day 61

*"Blessed are those who are persecuted
in the cause of right;
the kingdom of Heaven is theirs."*

Matthew 5:10, REB

If you've ever set up yourself to be a martyr, it's time to retire from that job! God does not impulsively send anyone to a cross. He wants you to admit your wants and wishes, and then be willing to lay down your desires and personal rights for His right of way. Such a decision may cause you slight discomfort or excruciating pain. God never asks His children to crucify themselves with their own hand.

In times of conflict, you just might find someone who's willing to nail you with threats, accusations, innuendoes, or blame. Although they won't be merciful, perhaps they'll be justified in their response! Perhaps not. Either way, such battle scars necessarily don't come from "the cause of right," and they're all wrong.

Conflicts inflict injury to both parties until healing peace prevails. The persecution to be suffered for righteousness' sake will not even involve what you want for your own sake! It's not your cause you take up. It's the be-cause of Jesus Christ: Because you're His, you cannot keep silent about Him. Because you believe in His redemptive power, you need not struggle in your own. Because you know what's right in God's sight, you aren't blinded by impure motives shown for what they are by His revealing Word. Because you're not a retired resident of God's kingdom, you won't ignore your responsibility to *be* on behalf of Christ!

Prayer: Dear Heavenly Father, help me not to wage an unholy war for my own "righteous" cause or anyone else's. Help me to hear Your commands and carry out Your orders without looking for an escape route! Help me always to be bold, obedient, and blessed with prayer as I embrace salvation in Christ's name.

Journey with God: What risks are you willing to take for God? Is peace and quiet at stake? Are you willing to jeopardize your possessions and risk being misunderstood or mistreated because of your belief in Christ and His belief in you? Don't risk jumping ahead of God's direction for you to be or do! Ask to see His blessed boundaries for your actions. Ask to know His blessed cause for you to be in His kingdom.

_____

_____

_____

_____

_____

_____

_____

_____

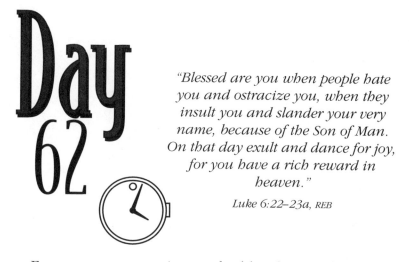

Day 62

"Blessed are you when people hate you and ostracize you, when they insult you and slander your very name, because of the Son of Man. On that day exult and dance for joy, for you have a rich reward in heaven."

Luke 6:22–23a, REB

For many years you've worked hard to establish your job credentials or reputation in the business world. If you've lived in one area for a while, you probably enjoy a good standing in your community. Maybe you're even known as "a pillar of the church." So you may not want people to think you're off your beam now!

A disadvantage of getting older is being immediately suspect! For instance, instead of making allowances for your mental occupations, people may now think you're "losing it!" If your mind happens to wander or if you can't quickly close the gap in the sentence you started, they'll wonder if you're "all there." Although, like most people, you've occasionally lost your train of thought, others may fear you've now lost your mind! If you also choose to spend your retirement hours conversing with God, you might have the added distinction of becoming known as a "religious nut!"

There is, however, advantage in being older. Eventually, you realize, "I don't care what people think!" The purpose is not to accentuate eccentricity but to retire yourself from the hold that people's opinions have on you. As you come to care less and less about what others think and more and more about what God thinks, you'll risk being hated, insulted, ostracized, penalized, and persecuted for what you believe. Maybe no one will listen to you, but you'll readily hear God.

You'll *believe* and *receive* what His Word says as true. You might lose your reputation or credibility, but you'll rejoice in this reward: to be in the blessed company of God's Holy Spirit and all peoples who celebrate Christ's name.

Prayer: Dear Lord, help me to be a party to Your will for Jesus' sake.

Journey with God: Party time! You're cordially invited to join the celebration of all who suffer in Christ's name. To be blessed with good company in your retirement, ask God to show you where to find such persons locally—perhaps in your home, your church, the political arena, a shelter, or the nearest jail.

_____

_____

_____

_____

_____

_____

_____

_____

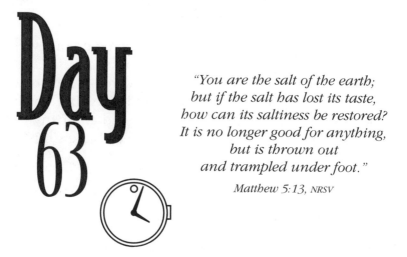

*"You are the salt of the earth;
but if the salt has lost its taste,
how can its saltiness be restored?
It is no longer good for anything,
but is thrown out
and trampled under foot."*

Matthew 5:13, NRSV

Do you ever see someone older get ignored, pushed around, or walked on? Do you fear being overrun yourself? People in a hurry sometimes act inconsiderately. Sometimes the rudeness physically endangers another person. If that's happened to you, perhaps you feel like staying home forever, but don't!

In Christ, you are the salt of the earth. You don't need to be thrown out as useless or trampled underfoot by careless people who rush to do what they want instead of following God. You follow Jesus. Therefore, you're free to be His mover and shaker of freely flowing salt!

Too much saltiness makes you a crusty old bird! Too little makes you nonirritating but bland. In Christ, you're both or neither! He knows when there are too few grains to make any difference, but He also knows how much it takes to make blood pressure rise in you or someone else. If you tried to distribute the precise amount of salt needed for each situation or person, you wouldn't know where to begin. You could not count the immeasurable significance of a single salty grain.

As Christ's Beatitudes become ingrained in you, His own flavor and favor enhance you. Your thoughts, attitudes, and actions become His. Your saltiness savors His good will and purpose for you. Therefore, this salt has no substitutes, nor can it be bought at any price. This salt springs not from yourself, but from close contact with the precious water and blood which flowed from the pierced hands and side of your Lord and Savior, Jesus Christ.

Prayer: Oh, Lord, keep me close beside You in the power of Your Spirit: the life-giving water and blood of Jesus' name.

Journey with God: Have you been baptized into Christ? Have you been looking for a salt substitute? Ask God to reveal His seasoning within you. Ask where, when, and how much salt He wants you to distribute to the people He brings to your mind. Ask for the salt of Christ to rub off onto you and onto others.

_____

_____

_____

_____

_____

_____

_____

_____

_____

_____

Day 64

*"You are the light of the world.
A city that is set on a hill
cannot be hidden."*

Matthew 5:14, NKJV

After the daybreak of His Beatitudes, Jesus concluded by saying, "You *are* the light." Before you do anything for God, He wants you to let the radiance of who you are dawn on you fully. He wants you to see that, as surely as the sun rises, you're called to be God's light. By yourself, though, you'll be little more than a flicker.

If you've been trying to show family or friends that you can make retirement work for you all by yourself, forget it! You can't. First, you need God as the source of your illumination and power. You need His strength, His wisdom, His light, and not your own. You need Him to show you clearly how to be in Him. Then, just as you think you see, He reminds you that it takes more than one person to be a city, to be a family, to be a retirement community, to be a church.

Without God and without other people, you're in the dark, alone. Maybe you'll be enlightened, but you won't light up anything or anyone, not even yourself. You won't see who you really are in Christ nor will you be able to show His light to others. You can try to get yourself all fired up, but you won't be ignited with any real sense of purpose. You just can't keep on fanning flames of enthusiasm by yourself.

You need *to be* with God. You need to be with other people, and they need your close company too. See? There's no substitute for Christ—or for you. Only you can be who only you can be. Yet it's not too bright to think you're all right and all light by yourself! So don't hide from the world, but neither let its darkness make you blow a fuse! Connect into Christ's levity around you. Join the joyous, burdenless, lighthearted illumination of Jesus' name.

Prayer: Dear God, thank You for the lightheartedness You bring in the company of other people who love You. Praise You for Your wisdom in revealing the light of Christ.

Journey with God: As it dawns on you who God wants you to be, you may be ready to plug into outlets for Christian service. Ask what He has in mind for you to do.

_____

_____

_____

_____

_____

_____

_____

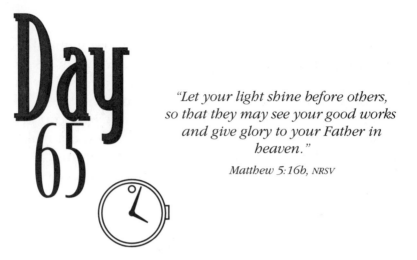

Day 65

"Let your light shine before others, so that they may see your good works and give glory to your Father in heaven."

Matthew 5:16b, NRSV

When you were a child or young adult, did anyone ever call you a show-off? Did you love getting accolades or being on center stage? Or were you so timid that you didn't want to show your personality, talent, or intelligence to anyone?

Did you hate being called on to lead a group or deliver a speech? Did you turn red-faced or brightly glow with each new spark of attention? Either way, guess what? You have a hindrance to overcome: *whatever you prefer to do!*

Most people usually love or hate to be in the forefront, but neither affects Christ's request. He did not ask your preference. He just said do it! Whether you like to shine or not is irrelevant, but you do have a choice. If you refuse, you won't be snuffed out! Yet you will miss a blessing—not just for yourself, but also for the people who might otherwise see God's good work in you.

As you reflect on your reflection—the light of Christ—you have multiple choices: (*a*) you can keep Christ hidden in your life; (*b*) you can try to outshine Him and everyone else; or (*c*) you can agree to be a Holy Spirit production of God's work in you. Do you see (c) as the only real choice? If so, great! Jesus doesn't ask your preference, but He does ask your permission! He said to *let* your light shine. He wants you to *allow* His shining to come through as you show who you are and what you do in Him. He won't force you to radiate. Rather, He wants you to be willing to step into whatever spotlight God places on you—not to be on show yourself, but so you will reflect your Father in heaven.

Prayer: Dear Lord, forgive me for being concerned about how well I appear to others instead of how well I reflect You. Help me to do as You ask and show Your love in Jesus' name.

Journey with God: How do you look at the light? Do you think its brightness conceals your flaws or reveals someone else's? Ask God to spotlight whatever keeps you from showing Him to others or giving Him glory for any good thing found in you.

_____

_____

_____

_____

_____

_____

_____

Day 66

"You hypocrite, first take the log out of your own eye, and then you will see clearly to take the speck out of your neighbor's eye."

Luke 6:42b, NRSV

To be light, you must *see* light—first in God, then in His children's reflection of Him. As you travel or become involved in new activities, you'll have contact with people you hadn't met before you retired. Often, you'll notice God's light through the glow on a face or reflection of love in an unusually radiant smile. Such signs of light set God's people apart from those who don't know Him. Such signs shine in you!

As you make new friends or get to know old ones better, you'll also see dark flecks in a person's eyes or character. Of course, they could say that about you too! Even the purest glass occasionally needs cleaning, and so does the purest heart. Meanwhile, streaks, spots, or dirt can show without the person even realizing that they are there. It may be up to you to tell them, but you won't be able to do so in a loving manner if you have trouble seeing yourself!

To see clearly, first get the log out of your own eye. This may be an unconfessed sin or an old account of someone else's trespass against you. Quickly dispose of those records! Otherwise, the log you keep on your mistakes or those of other people will also keep you from Christ's forgiving love. With confession and forgiveness, however, the ledger closes on each sin. Then you can see clearly! Then you reflect the loving light of Jesus' name.

Prayer: Dear Lord, I can easily see that other people's flaws and mistakes sometimes cast shadows on their work, but I don't like to think it affects mine! It's not my work that's dimmed, but Yours in me. Forgive me, Lord, for letting my record-keeping get in the way of Your light. Help me turn over each leaf of my ledger to You in the forgiving power of Jesus' name.

Journey with God: Have you kept accounts regarding who you are or what you do for God? Have you taken note of someone else's motives or behavior? Using the space below, let God audit your books! Let Him set each record straight as you confess, repent of record-keeping, and then forgive.

_____

_____

_____

_____

_____

_____

_____

_____

_____

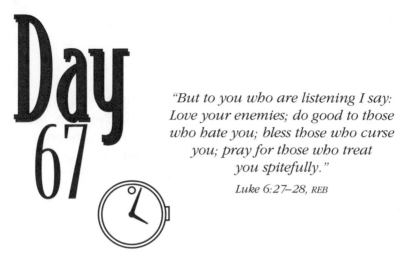

Day 67

"But to you who are listening I say: Love your enemies; do good to those who hate you; bless those who curse you; pray for those who treat you spitefully."

Luke 6:27–28, REB

Are you listening? Do you hear? Have you been allowing God time to speak to you each day as you read the Bible, pray, and journal? If so, congratulations! You've successfully begun your first weeks of retirement by hearing how *to be* in Christ. Now you're ready to learn what God wants you *to do*.

For many people, doing comes easier than being. Sometimes that's more pronounced when you first retire because you want to know that you can still contribute. If you felt pushed into retirement, the fear of being obsolete or ineffective can be so burdensome that you might want to hurry off to work somewhere simply to prove yourself. Yet the only thing you need to prove is your willingness to be in God and to do as He asks. First, this means listening, then obeying.

When you're ready to be involved in new activities, you might not do as you expect! Instead of rushing to a mission field or other worthy cause, God asks you to start *being* and *doing* at home or very nearby. How near? As beside yourself as you are to an unconfessed sin or as near as you are to a neighbor you dislike. . . . Somewhere in the proximity of your shortcomings and those of other people, you begin to do as Christ asks. For example, that rough-looking kid who gestures obscenely or that person who called you an unprintable name are in the mission field God has given you. So pray for people you disapprove of, disagree with, or detest. "God bless" them. To enemies, show love, not fear. Since you can't begin to do this alone, you need to be empowered by God to be able to obey Him. So *be*. Listen. Hear, and you'll know perfectly well what God wants you to *do!*

Prayer: Dear God, I don't want to love my enemies! I'd rather throw bricks, but I really don't want them thrown back. Help me to do as You've asked for Your sake, my enemy's sake, and my own sake too. Help me to love, bless, and pray for those who need all Your help they can get in Jesus' name.

Journey with God: Discuss with God anyone who has mistreated you. In obedience to His Word, rather than your feelings, forgive, bless, and pray for each person by name.

_____

_____

_____

_____

_____

_____

_____

Day 68

*"Ask, and it shall be given to you;
seek, and you will find; knock,
and it will be opened to you."*

Matthew 7:7, NKJV

With retirement did you close the door on work? Or did you begin to seek new employment immediately? Are you knocking yourself out now, trying to find someone to hire you?

If you really need to work, pray about it first. Seek God's will in the matter. Find the door He opens for you and don't knock any new opportunity! You may not have the opening you wanted, but you can trust that the work will work for you when you've first sought God's will!

Prayer is the key that is provided for opening doors. Before you insert that key, decide which door you'll pick. Will you choose Door 3 where your name is printed in bold gold letters and where you find lots of enticements? Will you pick Door 2 where other people think you should apply yourself? Or will you let God guide you into His will even if you have no job title, no job description, nor a clue!

To step through Door 1, you don't ask for what you want. The key comes in asking God what *He* wants you to request! He already said His will would be given to you, but He wants you to seek it, to know when it's found. So you pray, "Lord, please tell me what You want me to ask for. Show me Your will." Then *believe* He'll do just that! Wait for Him to bring His key thought and to lock in a new set of circumstances.

Suddenly, everything will just click! A door will open up to new possibilities and you'll walk through, confident to say, "I know this is God's will for me!"

Prayer: Dear God, I don't want to ask for anything You don't want because I just might get it! Please remind me that Your will is mine for the asking. Help me to have discernment so I can follow Your lead in Jesus' name.

Journey with God: Listen to what God has to say to you about these matching pairs of prayers: Ask = Receive. Seek = Find. Knock = Be Open. For instance, are you asking and receiving His requests of you? Are you being open to Him?

Day 69

"In this manner, therefore, pray:
'Our Father in heaven,
Hallowed be Your name.'"

Matthew 6:9, NKJV

As you pray about a job or the work you're to do, they just might be the same, depending on your unique situation. Having a job, however, doesn't mean necessarily you'll have an income any more than having an income always means you have a job! The two may be entirely different matters, so you might separate them in prayer. For instance, if you lack sufficient income, ask God to show you His solution or provision. If you need something interesting to do, ask God to reveal His will for your daily occupation of thought or use of time.

Whether you need a minimum wage, maximum income, or no additional earnings, you have work to do— a work of prayer. God hired you for that task when you became a Christian! So don't let another work distract you from this occupation. Throughout each day and evening, be on your job—praying.

In Christ, you are a *pray-er!* Therefore, you'll want to know how to be an effective one. You'll want to know how to do it the way Jesus did. Isn't that what happens when you start any job? You shouldn't have to guess what's expected of you. Someone needs to show you, and that's what Jesus did in the Lord's Prayer.

As you go about your daily work of prayer, follow His example. Begin with hallowing God's name. Honor, respect, and revere it. Think about it. Be in awe of His holiness, knowing you have none apart from Him. Admire God. Be impressed by Him! In a Bible concordance, look up "God's Names" or "Titles of God." Seek information from His Word. Find out who He was, is, and will be forever. Let aspects of His character become better known to you as you become opened to Him in prayer.

Prayer: Dear Father in heaven, how greatly You are to be praised! Lord, Your perfection awes me. Your mercy comforts me. Your truth impresses me. Your righteousness sets me apart and upright. Your forgiveness heals me. Your Spirit guides me, but I especially love Your love as shown in Jesus' name.

Journey with God: Take Christ at His Word! Personalize each line of communication with God as you take Christ's example to pray about your needs and others He places on your mind.

_____

_____

_____

_____

_____

_____

_____

Day 70

*"Your kingdom come.
Your will be done on earth
as it is in heaven."*

Matthew 6:10, NKJV

Had any big revelations lately? If you've enrolled in an adult class at church or a Bible study group in someone's home, you've probably heard people talking about Christ's return. Some hope He'll arrive before next month's bills come due. Others eagerly search the Book of Revelation to discover classified information about the job they might have. Still others get so upset at the possibility of change or suffering that they avoid reading God's Book to keep from knowing how it ends.

Occasionally, debates arise to accommodate each person's view. Quarrels erupt from ignorance, and misunderstandings occur when someone takes a verse out of scriptural context. Depending on what they want to hear, people may take a strong stand while you feel like retiring from Bible study forever! Instead, ask God to bring light onto a puzzling verse or a perplexing passage, and guess what? He will!

Through the power of Christ, God sent His Holy Spirit to guide, instruct, and empower those who ask. Even if you can't possibly attend a Bible study, you have God's own Holy Spirit to tutor you. In the spirited company of other godly Christians, you'll often have lively, challenging discussions and deeper insights into God's character and will.

Alone or in fellowship with other Christians, you'll get to know God better as you read His Word. Through Bible study, you'll discover what He wants for you personally but also for the whole world. Cover to cover, God's Word uncovers Him and His plans! You'll learn what He specifically wants you to ask for as you read the Bible too. So before you pray for Christ to come and God's will to be done, don't assume you know what you're requesting! Ask Him, and you'll find out.

Prayer: Heavenly Father, sometimes I accept what I've learned or heard from other people without even wondering what You're trying to teach me! Help me to hear Your revelation of what I'm asking in the pattern, presence, and power of Jesus' name.

Journey with God: Pray for God to reveal His kingdom at work in and around you. Seek His revelation of what you're to pray about for each person in your Bible study group. Find and note His answers.

_____

_____

_____

_____

_____

_____

_____

Day 71

"Give us today our daily bread."
Matthew 6:11, REB

Has anyone left your church saying, "I'm just not getting fed"—or have you yourself thought about leaving for that reason? Perhaps this rationale on church rations might be best expressed by saying, "I'm getting fed up!"

Every church has its problems. Through your communion with other Christians and especially through the bread and wine of communion in Christ, you *are* getting fed! If there's insufficient prayer or inadequate feeding on God's Word though, your church could be spiritually malnourished.

Jesus said, "I AM the bread of life" (John 6:35). He referred to Himself as manna from heaven—the food of faith that kept God's people alive during famine-like conditions. Yet despite this blessed nurturing, they wandered in the desert, looking for meat, herbs, and spices. That hasn't changed. God's people still sandwich in Bible reading and prayer requests instead of leisurely dining with Him and receiving the day's manna.

Think of it in this way: Before mealtimes, you say grace, and that's what your prayer times should be—the grace before the main course of God's Word. As you read the Bible again and again, your thoughts become consumed by God's. He fills your spirit with His Holy Spirit and serves you a nurturing word. As you read, it may come to you to stop right then and pray—to have a dinner conversation with God. Or perhaps a word from the Psalms, Isaiah, or the Gospels will speak so clearly to your unique situation or concern that you'll claim those promises or prayers for your own. You'll personalize them as you put your name or someone else's into its place before tabling the discussion. By feeding your prayers with Scripture, you open a full menu of hope and promise. As daily bread, God's Word becomes *His food* for your spiritual thought and growth.

Prayer: Dear God, praise You for the sustenance of Your Holy Spirit and Holy Word. Help me to this feast in Jesus' name.

Journey with God: Have you devoured the whole Bible, straight through, as you would any meal? Ask God to give you a desire to read *all* of His nourishing Word. Pray to comprehend any meaty passage you haven't been able to stomach or digest.

_____

_____

_____

_____

_____

_____

_____

Day 72

*"And forgive us our debts,
as we forgive our debtors."*

Matthew 6:12, NKJV

"More power to you!"

Yeah, right. Nobody else listens to me, so I don't know why I thought God would.

To do an effective job as God's pray-er, you want to be sure nothing hinders your prayers. If you happen to seek your own will instead of God's, that doesn't necessarily hinder your prayers. It just sends them in the wrong direction! So as you pray, first pray to know what to pray, and then you will pray aright! Then to give more power to your prayer life, just give what needs forgiving.

Ask yourself these questions: *Have I retired old debts? Have I surrendered to God each situation or person that causes me discomfort or pain? Have I released old memories to Him? Have I been quick to confess my mistakes and forgive myself?*

Unfortunately, people often think of unforgiveness as a feeling or a response that they just can't help. In God's kingdom (for which you have been praying!), forgiveness steps into a spiritual realm: Forgiving is the way to be and the thing to do in Christ's kingdom. Forgiveness is to be given again and again as needed. How? By choosing to do just that!

Say, for example, that you've tried very hard to forgive someone, but the hurt still remains. Or maybe you're in an ongoing situation that continues to upset you, but you can't do anything to change it. So you pray, "God, I choose to obey you by forgiving in Jesus' name." Perhaps your feelings will immediately lighten. Perhaps they won't. Either way, you've done as God asked. The results are up to Him, not you. But watch out! Look for more power to you in prayer.

Prayer: Dear Holy Father, forgive me for not forgiving others who trespass onto my property, thoughts, opinions, feelings, emotions, moods, will, or rights. Thank You for crossing off my full debt to You in the holiness of Jesus' name.

Journey with God: What lines have you drawn around yourself that you don't want anyone to step over? In what ways do you step across the clear lines of God's will? Pray to see the boundless mercy you inherited from Christ—mercy that can reroute natural inclinations.

_____

_____

_____

_____

_____

_____

_____

Day 73

"And do not lead us into temptation."

Matthew 6:13a, NKJV

Wow! I sure am tempted to do that.

As you make decisions about what you're to do during retirement, let this be a clue: God tempts no one. He obviously does allow people to be tempted, or Jesus would not have mentioned this concern, much less prayed about it! Led by the Holy Spirit into the wilderness, Jesus faced three tempting choices. He could feed Himself and no one else. He could take His kingdom right then but lose the power needed for others to accompany Him. He could jump off a cliff and escape further temptations and suffering.

Throughout His ministry, Jesus endured and overcame the temptation to do as He wanted instead of following the will of His Father. He also overcame the temptation *to do nothing*—to decline the work to which He'd been called. Alone in the garden, He asked to be relieved of the duty and burden of crucifixion for the sins of the world. Three times He prayed, sweating blood before He could rise from His knees, ready to be all He was meant to be and to do as He'd been asked.

Because of Christ's triumph, you have His power to be and do as you've been asked. Yet you also face the choice He had: to be and do what you want *or* what God wants. With each temptation you're tempted to do your own will instead of your Heavenly Father's. You're also tempted to follow the will of other people or, somehow, to prove yourself to them. Again and again, this happened to Jesus. Again and again, He was asked to pass the test of Himself through wonders, signs, and submission to the powers that be. He chose to be obedient to His Father, however. He chose to do the will of God.

Prayer: Dear Lord, thank You for understanding everything I go through. Help me not to be tempted to struggle in my own power or to be led astray by anyone else. Help me surrender to the triumph found only in Christ's name.

Journey with God: Who do you believe God meant you to be? What do you think He wants you to do? Who or what are you most tempted to be or do instead?

_____

_____

_____

_____

_____

_____

_____

_____

_____

Day 74

*"And do not put us to the test,
but save us from the evil one."*

Matthew 6:13, REB

Have you been thinking about going back to school but fear that you won't pass the entry requirements? Are you frightened by the thought of taking tests, doing homework, or being in the company of other students who aren't even half your age? Or are you undaunted by the possibility of failure but dread instead what you'd be expected to do with a new success?

If you decide to return to college, you'll find other retirees who aim to get that long-awaited degree. Technical schools offer you options too, especially if you'd like to develop skills in computers, mechanics, electronics, or the commercial arts. Adult education programs may also appeal to you, particularly if you don't seek a new career but want to learn more about a topic you've always found interesting.

So, if you've been toying with the idea of going back to school, don't play with the thought. Pray about it! Change can be scary at first, but the hard test comes in discovering your priorities. For example, if a friend begs you to enroll in a course that doesn't really appeal to you, perhaps you'll be tempted to go just for the company. Or if you hear that a certain course would give you a highly marketable job skill, you might be tempted to enroll even though that's not the field to which you feel most drawn.

The test continues as you separate genuine interests and true ability from erroneous thinking, phony motives, or false lures. God doesn't want you to be fooled by false hopes, false promises, or false premises about yourself; but His enemy does! Don't fight it! Let God save you from the evil of any mistaken notion about who you are or what you're to do.

Prayer: Heavenly Father, help me to know Your perfect plan for me in Jesus' name.

Journey with God: To enroll in a course or training program, you may be asked for a driver's license, social security card, or other form of positive identification. In what ways do you positively identify with Christ? Ask God to show any mistaken identity or evil intent that works against His good purpose in you.

_____

_____

_____

_____

_____

_____

_____

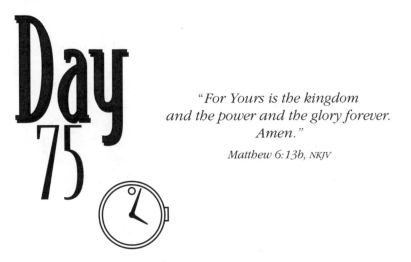

Day 75

"For Yours is the kingdom and the power and the glory forever. Amen."

Matthew 6:13b, NKJV

Is everything changing? Or is it just me?

During the first weeks of retirement, your old routines and priorities have undergone numerous alterations. Perhaps you have a different way of looking at things, too. Your focus has changed from earning a living to living an unearned life in Christ. You've retired from the pursuit of getting a raise or producing more business; now you regularly work overtime to practice journaling, Bible study, and prayer!

Some changes have been difficult; others have brought an immediate blessing. In some ways you're relaxed; in others you're alert as you discover more about yourself and God's will for you. You're also finding new insights into Him and His way of doing things. So you may feel upset if His Word seems to undergo alterations! For instance, as you look up a familiar verse in a modern translation, you may think, "Wait! That's not how it sounds! What happened? Is God changing too?" Of course not! People's perceptions of the Bible change as newer information or older manuscripts come to light.

For example, if you've read the Ten Commandments in a newer translation, you noticed it didn't say, "Thou shalt not kill," but instead, "Don't commit murder." Maybe you took that change in stride, but felt grieved by the omission of today's verse from most versions of the Bible. Apparently, ancient Greek manuscripts didn't contain the phrase, so the ending of that beloved prayer may have changed, but *Bible truth* does not: "Yours, O LORD, are the greatness, the power, the glory, the victory, and the majesty; for all that is in the heavens and on the earth is yours; yours is the kingdom, O LORD, and you are exalted as head above all" (1 Chron. 29:11, NRSV).

Prayer: Dear God, I'm glad You and Your truths don't change. Sometimes everything feels so unfamiliar to me, even myself! Help me to enjoy this retirement version of myself. Praise You for Your constant power and glory in Jesus' name.

Journey with God: Ask God what it means to be *His* version of you instead of your own interpretation or someone else's. In what ways does He want you to seek His power and glorify Him?

_____

_____

_____

_____

_____

_____

_____

Day 76

*But you are a chosen people,
a royal priesthood, a holy nation,
a people belonging to God,
that you may declare the praises
of him who called you out of
darkness into his wonderful light.*

1 Peter 2:9, NIV

If you're over fifty, you probably enjoy getting senior citizen discounts at hotels, restaurants, resorts, and other tourist attractions. If you're sixty-five or older, you might have medical benefits and other privileges, such as getting your college tuition paid at no cost to you. Advantages come as you get older. Others arrived the day you were born.

For instance, you have unique freedoms for just living in this country. Yet perhaps you had additional advantages in your upbringing. Maybe you had such a good job or made such good investments that you lack no material thing. Maybe you belong to a church or have good friends who welcome your calls or visits. Maybe you enjoy reasonably good health and a family who loves you even when you don't act too reasonably! Maybe you have so many talents and interests that you hardly know what to do with them or where to begin.

If you merely acquired your own kingdom, you might feel pretty proud of yourself! If you live in adverse conditions, however, you might feel resentful or envious of others. Yet, in God's kingdom, you dwell in a different state wherein all are equal. All have the same opportunity. All are gifted. All are blessed. All are special. All are chosen. All are eager to thank God, praise God, and give glory to God for all success.

God tells you clearly: You are chosen. Through Christ, you're robed in His finery, not your own. Regardless of age, sex, race, or earthly inheritance, you've been given God's Spirit freely and royally! You've been granted a holy estate—to be God's own child. Therefore, He gives you the special privilege to do the honors in bringing glory to His name.

Prayer: Dear Lord, praise You for bringing me out of my dark thoughts of pride, envy, or despair. Thank You for freely accepting and richly blessing me in Jesus' name.

Journey with God: For what do you feel chosen? What praiseworthy traits, talents, or special privileges can you declare as gifts from your Heavenly Father?

_____

_____

_____

_____

_____

_____

_____

_____

Day 77

"When you bear (produce) much fruit, My Father is honored and glorified; and you show and prove yourselves to be true followers of Mine."

John 15:8, AMP

I just can't bear this anymore.

Praise the Lord! You weren't supposed to bear anything alone, not even fruit! Unfortunately, many Christians swallow the pits instead of spitting out what bothers them! They send forth bruised or blighted fruit from their lips—grumblings or messages of dissatisfaction instead of fruitful prayer and praise. If that's what you've been doing, you undoubtedly have real cause for complaint. But will you rob God by withholding from Him the worry, fear, or anguish that burdens you?

Until you bury every seed of discontent or place every cutting of dissatisfaction into the Lord in prayer, you won't be able to see what springs forth as He produces good from this distress. You won't have any clear results of prayer for which to praise Him. Oh, He'll continue to weed and prune your life, but He won't harvest much appreciation or glory for all He's done to bless your spiritual growth.

Does it surprise you to know that your Heavenly Father receives abundantly from you as you sow each distress in Him? He's honored by a willingness to bear, not solitary burdens, but the sole fruit of His Spirit, produced by Christ in you. He doesn't want you to find such a life unbearable! Nor does He want you straining to bear pears when your grounds for complaint compost your life with lemon rinds! Heap every problem onto God and let Him produce a blessing for which you cannot help but bring forth praise.

Prayer: Dear Lord, forgive me for bearing burdens alone and being bowed down with problems instead of bowing in fruitful times of thanksgiving, prayer, and praise. Thank You for producing good results in me for Your glory in Jesus' name.

Journey with God: Is there something you just can't bear any longer? Discuss this with God. Ask Him to show you what it means to "lean on Jesus" for spiritual support and growth. Pray for the strength to let Christ bear your cross and to let yourself bear the fruit of His Spirit.

_____

_____

_____

_____

_____

_____

_____

_____

Day 78

"You did not choose me,
but I chose you and appointed you
to go and bear fruit—fruit that will
last. Then the Father will give you
whatever you ask in my name."

John 15:16, NIV

Good news! You've been chosen to be the recipient of other people's bad news! That's not intended to weigh you down by having you single-handedly take on other people's problems. Rather, as you lean toward Christ in prayer, you're inclined to be the bearer of other people's burdens to Him too. You've been chosen to be *fruitful* as you place each person or problem into prayer, trust God's good purpose, and point toward Him. Have you faithfully kept that appointment? Or are you afraid to ask God for anything for yourself or someone else for fear you just won't get it?

To avoid disappointment, first pray about what you're to do. Ask God how He wants you to respond to each situation. Ask what He wants you to pray about for each individual involved. Ask Him to fence off your thoughts and to hold back your fears from crowding in and getting in His way for you to pray. Then listen. Let His thoughts come to your mind. Let His Spirit direct yours into *His* prayer for you or someone else. Such moments of asking, seeking, and finding God's will for you to pray cannot help but open you up to spiritual productivity and highly fruitful results.

As God's choice fruit, share a prayer with others. Pray for them by yourself, especially if you're confined. Pray with them in private so they truly know your concern. Pray for them in public, as love and courtesy will allow, so you can inconspicuously display the fruitful life for which you have been picked.

Prayer: Oh, God, when a friend who was all upset called, did you pick me to pray? Whenever You appoint me to a task, help me not to disappoint You by failing to point other people toward You. Help me to lean on You in prayer in Jesus' name.

Journey with God: When you pray, what's really at stake? Do you lean toward rigid rules and duty or toward Christ to bear you with *His* prayer? Ask how to pray for yourself and others. Find out if your prayer "bin" is the Hebrew word, *bin*, which means discernment.

_____

_____

_____

_____

_____

_____

_____

_____

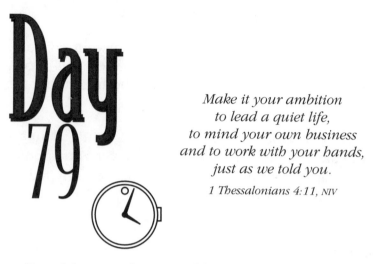

Day 79

*Make it your ambition
to lead a quiet life,
to mind your own business
and to work with your hands,
just as we told you.*

1 Thessalonians 4:11, NIV

"I *told* you this would happen if you didn't _____."

Now that you're retired, friends and family may act as though you have nothing to do but to listen to their problems! If so, that certainly does give you the opportunity to say what you think. If you have the advantage of white hair, you can be quite convincing as you spout forth wisdom on every topic. Yet get really wise; make it your ambition to mind your own business even though other people beg you to mind theirs!

If you don't handle this skillfully the first time or so you're asked an opinion, don't fret! Practice will perfect your ability to keep your lips sealed, knees bent, and hands at work in prayer. Alone, you might unclasp and spread your fingers as you submit private thoughts and opinions to the Lord. In the presence of an immediate prayer need, you might place a hand on someone's head, back, or shoulder. Then just pray quietly—so as not to scare them or yourself!

To *do* a good work of prayer, first learn to *be* quiet and listen. Offer no advice, but instead be busy in minding God's business for this person or situation. Say, "Let's pray about this right now." Then be ambitious about aiming your faith and prayers straight toward

God's will. *Be* quiet so you can hear His specific thoughts and opinion on how you're to pray. Then *do* it, just as He tells you.

Prayer: Lord, help me to get this prayer business straight. I'm to aim each person and problem directly toward You, not toward my own thoughts and opinions, right? OK, but if You want me to offer advice, please don't hesitate to ask! Of course, apart from You, I don't have anything to say about anything anyway. Forgive me for thinking I did. Help me to grow in wisdom, in strength, and in favor of Jesus' name.

Journey with God: Have you been trying to work out someone's problem by yourself? Have you spoken an untimely word or had an unseemly thought? Ask God if you're to seek forgiveness from someone He's handed to you for prayer. Pray for His word, wisdom, and discernment. Pray to hear what He's told you about having a quiet hand in His "business."

_____

_____

_____

_____

_____

_____

_____

_____

Day 80

Jesus answered,
"The work of God is this:
to believe in the one he has sent."

John 6:29, NIV

"It's a tough job, but somebody's gotta do it."

Praying for people can be quite a chore! For one thing, they seem to think you're on call anytime, day or night, and Sundays too. Before you know it, you're praying for someone during the last ten minutes of your favorite television show. You're praying on the phone and in your home. You're praying in a church aisle or in a grocery store parking lot.

As you quietly go about this business of listening to God and praying as He guides, you won't get spiritually worn out. At times, however, you might feel weary in body, mind, or emotions. You may suddenly realize you're so attuned to the Lord that you haven't heard a word someone is saying. You might start praying on the phone only to hang up with a crick in your neck. If you pray in person with a hand on someone's back or shoulder, you might get a pain in yours! So get comfortable before you start praying. If it takes a while, shift prayer positions. God won't be upset if you kneel, sit, or stand on your head—unless you lie down on the job and don't do it!

Praying for people can take a toll on you anytime, but especially when things *seem* to take a turn for the worse! So expect the unexpected. For example, if you pray as directed for someone's total healing, don't be shocked if that very night they die! Why? There's more than one method of healing, and death does completely heal. Fortunately, that's not your decision; it's God's. This is where the real work comes in, however, so fill your name into this Scripture: "The work of _____ is to *believe* in the one He has sent." Believe in yourself as the one sent to pray. Believe in the Lord as the One sent to answer each prayer as He knows best. Believe in other loving Christians whom God has sent to help and pray for you.

Prayer: Dear God, I thought it was hard overcoming timidity to pray for people. It's harder, though, to trust You. Forgive me for thinking I'm more concerned about someone's well-being than You are. Help me to leave the results in Jesus' name.

Journey with God: Have you confused your job with God's? Discuss this with Him.

_____

_____

_____

_____

_____

_____

_____

_____

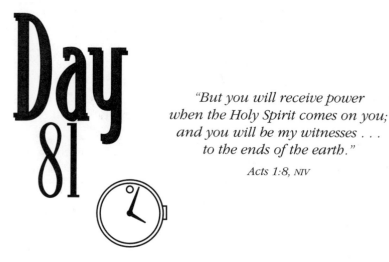

Day 81

*"But you will receive power
when the Holy Spirit comes on you;
and you will be my witnesses . . .
to the ends of the earth."*

Acts 1:8, NIV

Have you ever witnessed an accident or been immediately on the scene? If so, you might have been called upon to give a full statement, attesting to the facts as you saw them. Of course, this may not be exactly what someone else saw, heard, or believed. There may be some discrepancies, and yet each person tells nothing but the whole truth as they experienced it.

Sometimes, Christians try to witness *before* they have experienced anything of the Lord. They testify to hearsay based on other people's testimony. Under cross-examination, they may see that they've failed to give God the right of way. They may confess failure to fasten themselves to the cross, but having seen and heard nothing, they have nothing to tell.

If nothing's happened to you, don't hurry away hurt! Wait. Before you tell anyone about God, wait for the power of His witness. Wait for Christ's Holy Spirit to come upon your thoughts, mind, heart, and attitudes. Wait for the loving counsel of the Holy Spirit to lovingly correct, comfort, heal, and guide you safely into the jurisdiction of God's power. Let Christ be your advocate before the Heavenly Father as you advocate His principles and prayers before people. Let your "witness for

Jesus"—your testimony on Christ's behalf—be no accident, but the power He deliberately promised you.

Prayer: Dear Holy Father, I stand in awe of Your power. Oh, Lord, forgive me for colliding my will with Yours. Forgive me for being at cross-purposes with You when You tried to caution me or intersect my life. Forgive me for clashing with other people when I tried to direct them like traffic. Empty me of every self-centered, self-sufficient route. Clear all the debris from each collision and set me on my feet, upright in You. Show me Your way, Lord. Hold me in Your strength. Fill me with Your Holy Spirit and help me to welcome, receive, and testify to the driving force of Christ's name.

Journey with God: In what ways can you personally attest to the Holy Spirit's power in you?

_____

_____

_____

_____

_____

_____

_____

_____

For we cannot keep from speaking about what we have seen and heard. Acts 4:20, NRSV

"Wow! What a testimony!"

If you have dramatic evidence of God's work in your life, you have a lot to say! Even if you wanted to keep quiet, you couldn't. Perhaps you've seen God bring back life to people who were once depressed, drunk, or destitute. Maybe you've seen Him restore health, fortunes, and goodwill. Regardless, the more you've seen and heard, the more you have to tell. People won't always listen. Nevertheless, speaking about God is your job; getting them to hear is His!

Perhaps, though, you've had trouble hearing or seeing Him yourself. Were your ears opened to a Bible teaching, a timely word from a Christian friend, or God's inner voice within? Were your eyes opened to every page of His Word and each line of His work? Or were you afraid to watch? That's not uncommon. God's people begged Moses to wear a veil after being in His presence because they could not bear to see the radiance on his face. They also asked him to relate what he had heard, so they wouldn't have to listen to God themselves.

If you're fearful of seeing God's work or hearing Him yourself, perhaps you once glimpsed or overheard something you didn't like. That happens to everyone at

166

times, and yet, as you come to trust God more, you know you've no cause to be afraid. Nor do you have cause for anger if there's been some misunderstanding between you and Him. So make up with God! Then thank and praise Him for having holy power and using it in ways you can't begin to comprehend! Look. Listen. Keep seeking and speaking to God, and you'll find plenty to say!

Prayer: Dear Lord God, forgive me for wanting to confine You to my own understanding. Your power amazes me, yet scares me too. Sometimes I feel angry or hurt when You don't do as I've asked, and so I hesitate to pray for anything. It thrills yet frightens me when I see other people rescued by You, but I'm not always sure You see my needs or hear me. Help me witness Your love and the work of Your Spirit in Jesus' name.

Journey with God: What keeps you from hearing, seeing, and knowing God well enough to speak clearly about Him to others?

_____

_____

_____

_____

_____

_____

*But in your hearts set apart
Christ as LORD.
Always be prepared to give an
answer to everyone who asks you
to give the reason for the hope
that you have. But do this
with gentleness and respect.*

1 Peter 3:15, NIV

To be set apart for Christ, first set Him above you as Lord. In some ways this can be easier now since you no longer have an employer, business partner, deadline, or production level lorded over you! If you once had a powerful position in the business world, perhaps you thought you ruled a kingdom, but now you see that you don't.

Before letting Christ take His rightful place as Lord, you need to know that His lordship does not, as rumored, make Him your copilot, cocaptain, coworker, or partner. If He's truly your Lord, He's the only One in charge. He's the Chief, the King, the President, the Cornerstone of your life. He's the Commander, but not the demander.

As you tell others about the Lord, the Bible encourages you to be gentle and show respect. Why? Because that's how God treats you. Others may make demands, threats, or harsh accusations against you, but not God. For instance, when His Holy Spirit corrects or chastises you, it's with such tender regard that you just want to say, "Oh, I didn't realize I was doing that. Thanks for telling me." Likewise, God wants you to be lovingly respectful as you instruct others about Him. He wants you to know and show His love—His lordship that does not lord itself over you but invites you into His kingdom.

As you seek Christ's lordship, let your heart be willing to find yourself set apart as His disciple. Place your hope in God's wisdom and direction not just for your eternal life, but for each second, starting now! Ask the gentle, loving, and most respectful Christ to be your Lord. Then be prepared when others ask you all about Him.

Prayer: Dear God, I'm not prepared! I get so busy going my own way, I forget to seek Yours. Help me to follow Your love in all I am, say, and do in Jesus' name.

Journey with God: Who or what do you allow free reign over you? What real reason do you have to hope in God?

_____

_____

_____

_____

_____

_____

_____

_____

_____

Day 84

All this has been the work of God. He has reconciled us to himself through Christ, and has enlisted us in this ministry of reconciliation.

2 Corinthians 5:18, REB

As you seek Christ's lordship, you may realize that you have occasionally (not often, of course) lorded your view, opinions, possessions, profession, or obsessions over other people. Maybe you've playfully lorded your retirement over someone who has to wait a few more years. Everyone enjoys a taste of power, but to be a minister of reconciliation, you eventually must reconcile yourself to the lordship of Christ.

What does this mean? It may differ for individuals, yet the same questions remain: Who's the boss? Who chooses how you spend your time, talent, money, or energy? Who decides what you're to say or to refrain from saying? Who helps you to know when to hang on or let go? If you make all such choices without first consulting God, you've insulted His lordship.

In Christ, you are forgiven! Therefore, in Him, you're able to forgive. It's His love you offer, not your own. It's His evidence of caring, salvation, and holiness that you show. So be reconciled to your own limitations. Be willing to see that, apart from Christ, you have nothing good to show for yourself! Without Him beside you, you're beside yourself with worry, fear, pride, judgment, and self-condemnation.

Be reconciled to God's love, even when you act the least lovable! Be reconciled to Christ's reconciliation, between you and God, from the cross. In His strength, His power, and His Holy Spirit, you have the ability to be His minister to other people. You have the power not to do necessarily what you or others want, but what He asks. He asks you to pray for church and family members with whom you've disagreed so He can win them over with His love. He's your Lord, yet nothing is beneath Him! Come to Him with all of your otherwise irreconcilable differences.

Prayer: Dear Lord and Savior, I praise You for reconciling me to You, myself, and other people in Jesus' name.

Journey with God: What seemingly irreconcilable differences have you withheld from Christ's lordship? Exactly what isn't working in the work God wants to work in and through you?

_____

_____

_____

_____

_____

_____

_____

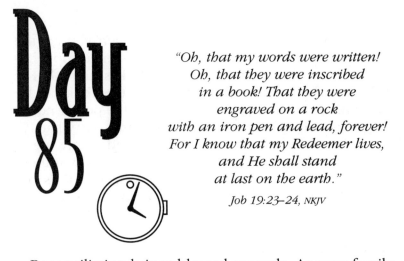

*"Oh, that my words were written!
Oh, that they were inscribed
in a book! That they were
engraved on a rock
with an iron pen and lead, forever!
For I know that my Redeemer lives,
and He shall stand
at last on the earth."*

Job 19:23–24, NKJV

Reconciliation brings blessed rewards. As your family and friends come together in agreement with God, you'll see harmonious accord such as you never thought possible. Yet, no matter how hard you try to reconcile the people you love or how lovingly you attempt to lead them to Christ, they might not be ready. The perfect, timely moment belongs to God. You might take time, however, to remind yourself about God's work in your life and eventually share this with others too.

To write *His-story* in you, start chronologically with the first time you remember hearing about God. Perhaps you recall a song such as "Jesus Loves Me" or recollect your nighttime prayers. If you have relevant photographs, such as a picture of the first church you attended, consider starting a scrapbook. Include the program, bulletin, or announcement of the day you were baptized. Type your favorite Bible verses and devotional thoughts or poems you've written.

If your family has a history of Christian faith, write down specific episodes and events. Should someone in your family be estranged from God or other Christians, write a letter expressing His love and yours. If that person happens to be upset with you, enclose a note of forgiveness too.

Perhaps you won't live to see full restoration of God's love within your family, but you can *know* His love still stands. One day every knee shall bow and every tongue shall confess Christ's lordship. A day will come when everyone in your family shall see God as He is. Meanwhile, let your profession of His love be written in you.

Prayer: Dear Lord, I praise You for coming into my home, church, and friendships. Thank You for making everything all right in Your perfect timing in Jesus' name.

Journey with God: In this space, jot down key phrases or words to help you recollect the thoughts and events you're to include in "The Family of Christ Album." Ask God to remind you.

_____

_____

_____

_____

_____

_____

_____

_____

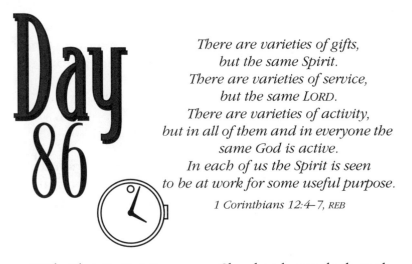

There are varieties of gifts,
but the same Spirit.
There are varieties of service,
but the same LORD.
There are varieties of activity,
but in all of them and in everyone the
same God is active.
In each of us the Spirit is seen
to be at work for some useful purpose.

1 Corinthians 12:4–7, REB

With Christ's Spirit as your Shepherd, you lack nothing that is needed for His service. If you need more rest, He provides it as you rest in Him and the promises of God's Word. If you're thirsty for truth, wisdom, love, companionship, or any good things of His Spirit, He quenches this need in such a quiet way that you needn't be afraid. He restores your soul and stores it unto Himself for eternal life in heaven and His own useful purpose here on earth.

You need God, but He also needs you. Look around, and you will see. The homeless, starving, orphaned, and lost people of this world—of your own community—do not even know of God's pastureland or quiet streams. God knows they're there, but they have no knowledge, no understanding of Him. So He looks to you to care. He looks to you to pray. He looks to you to comfort and guide these hurting people with the very comfort and guidance you've received abundantly from Him.

How many needs there are! How many Christians are there? How many useful purposes does Christ have in you? One Lord, one faith, and one baptism restore the souls of all His children. One Spirit is seen to be at work in you. Even if you cannot leave your house, you can be available for active service as God's Spirit moves you!

Perhaps He blesses you with a life of intercession from your bedside as He leads you beside still waters into prayer.

The LORD is my shepherd; I shall not want. He makes me to lie down in green pastures; He leads me beside the still waters. He restores my soul.

Psalm 23:1–3a, NKJV

Prayer: Holy Shepherd, thank You for filling my own needs with Your Spirit and empowering me to see my usefulness in helping others. Thank You for Your gentle nudge toward times of rest, times of nourishment, and times of activity as I'm so moved in Jesus' name.

Journey with God: Toward what useful purpose is God leading you?

_____

_____

_____

_____

_____

_____

_____

_____

_____

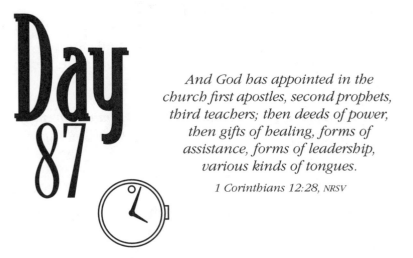

Day 87

*And God has appointed in the
church first apostles, second prophets,
third teachers; then deeds of power,
then gifts of healing, forms of
assistance, forms of leadership,
various kinds of tongues.*

1 Corinthians 12:28, NRSV

As you faithfully point yourself and others toward God, He will show His timely appointment for your retirement years.

Very likely, the work to which He presently calls you will be somewhere between a current need and your ongoing ability, awareness, or interest. For example, if you live in an area where no church exists, God may lead you to be an apostle as you establish a local gathering in Christ's name. If you attend a church founded by past generations, He might give you a prophetic word to strengthen and direct His people now. If you constantly read the Bible and can explain well your exciting discoveries, He may want you to teach.

As God leads you into the right path for you, He'll give you what you need to *be* and *do* all He asks. Consider then your own needs, past or present. For example, if you once needed a spiritual, emotional, or physical healing, God may empower you to provide His healing to others now as you lay a hand on them in prayer. If you needed financial assistance, He may give you enough to assist others too. If you needed to be led out of an abusive situation, He might counsel you in counseling. If He gave you a way with words, He might give you a word of encouragement, devotion, or praise to point others toward Jesus' name.

*He leads me in the paths of righteousness
for His name's sake.*

Psalm 23:3b, NKJV

Prayer: Heavenly Father, I praise You for filling my needs with Your strength and provisions. Thank You for directing me now toward others with whom I can share Your gifts. Help me not to rely on myself, but on You for the sake of Jesus' name.

Journey with God: What does your church, family, or community need the most? In what areas do you feel most drawn to help? In what ways has God already given you exactly what's needed for yourself and other people too?

_____

_____

_____

_____

_____

_____

_____

_____

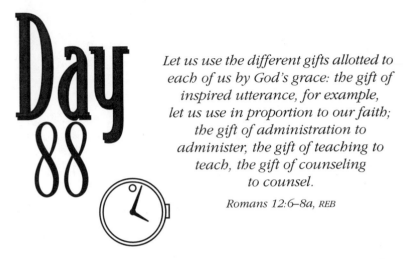

Let us use the different gifts allotted to each of us by God's grace: the gift of inspired utterance, for example, let us use in proportion to our faith; the gift of administration to administer, the gift of teaching to teach, the gift of counseling to counsel.

Romans 12:6–8a, REB

By God's grace, you're gifted! Isn't that amazing? Who but God would even think of taking what you lack to help fill necessities for other people? Yet that's often how God works. First He gives you what you need and then empowers you to render that gift to someone else. Using the comfort with which He's comforted you, you bring comfort to others. With the inspired word you receive from His Spirit, you then have something inspiring to say. With God's promises and instructive message from the Bible, you can teach what you know to be true.

Given, you're enabled to give, and yet so many retirees just feel "give out." Perhaps you do too. If so, let this be a clue that you're ready *to be filled*. This may be the Holy Spirit's filling, bracing you for active service in Christ's name. This may be God's filling you with a new direction, a new sense of purpose in Him.

Even if you constantly face the pain of your mortality, God stands beside you. His rod—His strong, unchanging rule over your spiritual life—continuously protects you from encroachment of evil. His faculties—His staff—provide what yours may lack. Such gifts come from the grace of God, but in return you give Him your faith. Trust Him. Rely on Him. Believe in Him and the powerful work He's given you to do.

Yea, though I walk through the valley of the shadow of death, I will fear no evil; For You are with me; Your rod and Your staff, they comfort me.

Psalm 23:4, NKJV

Prayer: Dear God, I feel so powerless! Without Your strength, I am. I thought retiring meant I could lie back with no more expectations on me, and yet that's boring after a while. I need to be needed, Lord. Oh, thank You! Praise You! Bless You for needing me in Jesus' name.

Journey with God: What do you least have to give? What help, counsel, or instruction has God administered "just in time" for your spiritual well-being? What gifts do you have that you know, without a doubt, come from Him?

_____

_____

_____

_____

_____

_____

_____

Day 89

If you give to charity,
give without grudging;
if you are a leader,
lead with enthusiasm;
if you help others in distress,
do it cheerfully.

Romans 12:8b, REB

What do friends and enemies have in common? They both follow you! Although you're retired from the business world, you may have some of both hanging around, waiting to see how you're doing. Would it surprise them if you bore forgiveness instead of grudges—if you came equally to either side in distress? Would they be shocked by your charitable attitude? Would they say, "This isn't the person I knew! This is a servant of the Lord"?

As you feed on love and forgiveness, God brings you to a banquet and places you alongside Himself. He anoints you for service with the oil of joy, the oil of gladness. He fills you with His Holy Spirit until His love, truth, and mercy can't help but spill onto those with whom you come in contact—friend or foe!

Do not think, however, that you can anoint yourself. Nor can you prepare a banquet in your own honor. Nor can you fill your own cup. God alone can do this. Only in His Spirit can you be *entheos,* "in God," with *enthusiasm.* Only in Him can you be led in the right direction for yourself and others. Only in Him can you cheerfully provide what He's freely given you.

You prepare a table before me in the presence of my enemies;
You anoint my head with oil; my cup runs over.

Psalm 23:5, NKJV

Prayer: Oh, Lord, I've been trying to work up my enthusiasm for something ever since I retired! I've surrounded myself as best I can with friends and family—I know they love me—but everyone has so much to do. Sometimes they seem too busy for me, and that hurts; but I know self-pity hurts me more. My own dark thoughts become my enemy! Yet You sit down beside me. You come to me. You prepare for me. You fill me with Yourself. Help me to receive You, Lord, and overflow with Your love in Jesus' name.

Journey with God: What enemies keep you from receiving more of God? What distress can you cheerfully give Him?

Day 90

You are, I know, eager for gifts of the Spirit; then aspire above all to excel in those which build up the church.

1 Corinthians 14:12, REB

As you go forth into God's blessings for retirement, your friends, family, and even your enemies might not always be close to you. If those nearest and dearest to you have already died, you might be feeling as though there's nothing ahead for you but loneliness, pain, and suffering. In especially dark moments, you might wonder where God is. Perhaps you'll doubt His presence.

You're not alone. Other Christians—even those who seem strongest in their faith and most active in their church—feel this way at times. In the Bible, however, you'll find a constant source of comfort, energy, and strength. A psalm, a verse from the Gospels, a timely word from God's Word will give your faith a lift; and you will see Him as He is—beside you in Spirit and in truth.

Surely, God's goodness and mercy will follow you all the days of your life. Surely, He will upbuild you and help you to upbuild His church. In the sanctuary of your home or your church, God asks you to get together with other Christians in Christ's name. As you gather in His Holy Spirit, you have all that's needed *to be* in Him and *to do* as He has asked. With eagerness, receive. Live by faith with thanksgiving. Praise God for your needs and for your gifts. Use what you've been given in service to Him and His people. As He dwells in you more fully, you more fully will dwell in Him. With or without your body's housing, be assured of this: you will continue to live and serve forever in the house of the Lord.

Surely goodness and mercy shall follow me all the days of my life; And I will dwell in the house of the LORD forever.

Psalm 23:6, NKJV

Prayer: Precious Lord and Savior, let me dwell with You for better or for worse, for richer or for poorer, in sickness and in health, to love and to cherish, as long as I shall live—forever in Christ's name.

Journey with God: Oh, listen! God's Word of your perfection and completion comes from His own Spirit as He says: "Well done, My good and faithful servant!" Pray to see what you have yet *to be* and yet *to do* in Him.

_____

_____

_____

_____

_____

_____

_____

_____

_____